No-Stress Retirement
Roadmap

No-Stress Retirement Roadmap

D. Scott Kenik

ASD Publishing

© 2023

No-Stress Retirement Roadmap

ISBN 978-0-9762806-1-3

Printed in the USA

"Compound interest is the eighth wonder of the world.
He who understands it, earns it...he who doesn't...pays it."

— Albert Einstein

When you transition from work to retirement,
your entire life changes, especially your finances.

You are no longer contributing to your savings;
you are now withdrawing.

When you reach that stage, you need to think
differently about your money.

Your financial goals should shift
from accumulation with risk,
to protection and income.

— D. Scott Kenik

TABLE OF CONTENTS

Preface

When I started in financial services back in 1995, I aspired to help clients find the best health, life, and disability insurance. After several years of making sure the rubber met the road, I was recruited by an administration service company to teach financial advisors from Merrill Lynch, Morgan Stanley, Prudential, and other national companies about how to use custom-written 401(k) plan designs, rather than using cookie cutter plans, to dramatically increase tax savings.

I worked with new representatives as well as seasoned advisors, and I was surprised to realize how little these representatives knew about how the plans they offered to their clients worked. The representatives reminded me of the neighborhood insurance agent who sold homeowners', auto, boat, RV, motorcycle, and basic life insurance. All too often, rather than delving deep into product design and benefits, they skimmed the surface and offered just the basics. As generalists, they often knew a little about a lot of things, but not much about any one product or service.

This experience planted a seed for me. I decided that from that point forward, I would make sure I would educate myself and my clients to provide them most value possible.

After a stint at Metropolitan Life, where I helped launch a new retirement program, I decided to open my own practice and specialize in retirement planning for clients near retirement and in retirement. By this point in my financial services career, I believed there should be a major difference in financial planning between the accumulation phase—the working years—and the distribution phase—retirement. All too often, I was seeing there was little to no difference. But I knew that when one retired, there needed to be a change in how they thought about money and income.

This is the genesis of *No-Stress Retirement*. This book is all about making sure that you can truly enjoy your retirement without stressing about money.

1 A No-Stress Retirement Is Possible

It turns out that my parents had a very stressful retirement. They spent much of their retirement taking seminars and learning about investing in the stock market and they traded their own accounts to supplement their retirement income. As far as I knew, they were successful. They never said otherwise.

But when my dad passed, my mom admitted to me that they had lost a lot in the stock market, and she was concerned about having enough money to live on. I want to point out that they were both smart people and had dedicated a lot of their time to learn about investing. But she was right. They didn't have enough to thrive in retirement as they had hoped. Instead of Mom enjoying her golden years, she had to pinch every penny hoping that her money will last.

When the economic crash happened in 2008, prompted by the mortgage crisis, I watched my retirement account drop like a rock, as did my friends and associates.

I knew there had to be a better way.

In these unprecedented times of high volatility, people watch helplessly as their retirement plan balances plunge. For many, these losses mean that they can no longer afford to retire or stay retired. Among them are those who have lost spouses and those who have no financial plan at all.

These financial problems wouldn't have happened if retirees had structured a proper retirement plan that shielded them from market losses and provided lifetime income.

In our younger working years, our goal is accumulation and growth of our hard-earned money. The best place for that, with the right guidance, is the stock market. We can afford market risk, and we can even afford market crashes since we have our paycheck. During this phase, we still have many years before retirement; we don't need the money, yet. We have time to allow the stock market to break even some years, recover other years, and grow in the long run.

But—and this is a big "but"—those favorable elements are gone when we are near retirement or in retirement. When retired, instead of contributing to the plan, we are withdrawing, and a market crash can devastate a retirement nest egg. I have witnessed what a stock market downfall can do, and I've met with far too many retirees who needed to get a job during retirement to cover the lost income from their accounts. I have also talked to retirees that had to downsize their homes or stop their travel plans because they could no longer afford their expenses, never mind their dreams. Worse yet, I've had to walk through the grief of those who lost their home in the last market crash. These are moments you don't wish upon anyone. Yet they are happening to some of the nicest people.

*It's great to have a job in retirement if you **want** to work, but it's quite another to **have** to work in retirement*

When you shift from your working years to your retirement years, your life and your finances change. And with those changes there needs to be changes in your financial plan. You should no longer chase growth with maximum risk, because that risk is real. Market crashes are real. Instead, your goal should shift to protection and income.

No-Stress Retirement Means ENJOYING Life.

This is where my *No-Stress Retirement* plan comes into play. So, what does "no-stress" retirement mean?

I look at a life plan in much the same way that I look at a week on the calendar. In our working years, we toil five days a week at our jobs to enjoy two days on the weekend.

Our money goes to our mortgage, food, car payments, taxes, insurance, clothes, gas, and so much more. The list seems almost endless. Along the way, there's college to pay for and we squirrel away what's left over for a rainy day and even some for retirement. Earning and saving enough for bills plus having enough money to raise a family can be stressful.

And then, if life permits, we make it to retirement. So, like the work week of five days to enjoy two, we've now spent 45 years working to enjoy 20 or so years of retirement. The key word here is, hopefully, "enjoy."

What makes retirement enjoyable? For me, "enjoying" retirement means having enough money to do anything you want without having to worry about where the money will come from.

As University of Wisconsin-Milwaukee's Professor Bender observed In the Wall Street Journal article "The Secret to a Happier Retirement," retirees who receive traditional company pensions are happier than those who have to rely solely on the savings they have amassed in 401(k) and similar retirement

savings plans.[1] Understandably, seniors like the sense of
security that comes with guaranteed, predictable income.

That last sentence describes exactly what our *No-Stress
Retirement* plan is all about. We create a financial plan that
can guarantee you income, like a pension, and that income
should be enough to cover your expenses, goals, and dreams
in an account that can never drop due to stock market crashes.
That way you never have to worry about paying your bills or
doing the things you enjoy for the rest of your life. You can go
to sleep and wake up in the morning without worrying about
money. I call it sleep insurance.

You have insurance on your house, you have car insurance, and
you have health insurance. Shouldn't your retirement also be
insured? Read on to find out how you can accomplish precisely
that and achieve the best sleep you've ever had.

2 Retirement May Cost More Than You Expect

I am often surprised at the income expectations some clients say that they expect they will need during retirement. All too often they tell me that they expect to only need half of what they are currently earning. They figure that the kids will be out of the house, and the mortgage will be paid.

To this, I mention two things that they may not be considering: inflation and the true cost of retirement. I will talk about inflation in the chapter, *The Four Greatest Wealth Killers*. For now, let's spend a moment discussing the hidden costs of retirement.

In your working years, you are earning money five days a week and spending money two days a week. Sure, you are spending money all week, but most people will recognize that the bulk gets spent on the weekends or away from work, when we socialize, travel, go on dates, or take the family out for dinner.

Contrast that with retirement, when you are no longer working. At this stage in your life, your wages disappear and in the place of an honest living, you are now spending money seven days a week. You can't watch TV and tend the yard all day, so you go out and do things. Put simply, you have more opportunities to spend money. And most people do.

Maybe you are fixing things on the "honey-do" list. Maybe you are meeting friends for coffee or having a few beers with the gang. Perhaps you miss your old colleagues at work and invite a few to meet for lunch. Others prioritize visiting family that they haven't seen in years. Or they go on an antique quest, golf, fish, or just take a joy ride. Let's not forget the visits to the kids and grandkids, the vacations, and just errands around town. These all cost money, and on top of that, the gasoline costs add up quickly.

Let's take a look at some of those assumptions. Sure, the kids are gone, but so are your child tax credits. This raises your taxes. Meanwhile, most people aren't really "saving" now that their kids are out of the house. They are instead redirecting those expenses to grandkids through visits, gifts, and help with college costs.

Turning to that perceived benefit that you have paid off your mortgage, the reality is you've also lost your interest deduction. That's another hike in your taxes.

And now that you are home more, what are the chances you will see "needed" renovations? I spent a fortune renovating my bathrooms and refinishing the kitchen cabinets. Perhaps you will decide to purchase that lakeside house you have dreamed about, or a vacation home, boat, new car, or an RV. The fact is there is no end to the things you can justify purchasing once you hit retirement. "You can't take it to the grave," right?

Unfortunately, some additional factors that will play a role. Each year, health insurance tends to cover less, yet out-of-pocket expenses and policy costs rise. The older we get, the more complicated our care gets. That inevitably leads to higher medical costs. And if, God forbid, we have to consider nursing care or long-term medical care, you can add a few zeros to that cost of care.

When clients tell me that they will only need 50% of their current income when they retire, I ask them if they have factored all these "additional" expenses into their estimate. I'm sure that you can guess their answers.

A proper *Fill-the-Gap* plan will allow for your current costs, inflation, and both planned and unplanned expenses in retirement.

3 The Four Greatest Wealth Killers

The road before retirement is bumpy and can rattle your fenders, but if you hit those same bumps during retirement, you'd better be prepared, otherwise those fenders may just break loose. I say this because while you are in your younger working years, you are still contributing money to your account and you don't yet need the money. Therefore, you'll have time to weather the bumps and storms before you'll need to withdraw money for your retirement. But during retirement, when the time comes that you need that money to pay bills and enjoy life, those same bumps could turn into wealth killers.

And though I wish I could say there's just one potential wealth killer, the fact is there are many that may rear their ugly heads. The three biggest wealth killers are market risk, taxes, and fees. But more recently, a fourth grim reaper has started sucking the life out of retirement accounts—and that is inflation. You may have thought you planned things perfectly, but when you run out of money because things cost 30% more than expected while your investments simultaneously shrink, plenty of well-meaning and well-planned people find themselves in a panic. The purpose of this chapter is to give you some insight in addressing all four of these potential and real disasters.

Wealth Killer #1: Market Risk
Let's start off with the greatest of wealth killers: market risk.

As I write this, we are coming off of one of the longest bull markets in history. Few of us have the fresh recollection of losing half of our wealth in a matter of days, and as a result, many investors have forgotten about market risk and crashes. The frightening fact is that during the 120-year history of the market, it has crashed an average of every 11 years and it loses 47% on average during those crashes!

Right now, we are way past that 11-year average. Based on the market's history, we expect a significant crash to be imminent; we just don't know when it will happen.

We all agree that the stock market will eventually recover—it always does. But historically, it has taken an average of about 6.2 years just to break even after a crash. That's a significant lost opportunity cost for anyone who experiences it. "Lost opportunity cost" simply means the cost of not being able to do the things you want such as earn interest or buy the goods you would like to have.

You may have heard the expression: "It's just a paper loss, the stock market will come back." This may be true, but when the market does start gaining again, your principle—the money you hope to earn profits on—is now a fraction of what it once was. That is a huge setback. Instead of capitalizing on six years of growth, you will spend those same six years just hoping to get back to where you were.

Consider the following table showing the history of the market from 1930 to present: The losses incurred in the down years of the market could easily devastate a retirement account.

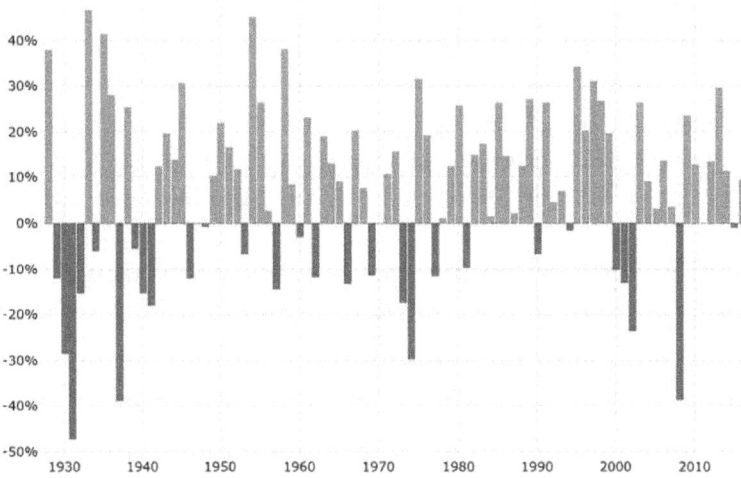

Take a look at this listing of the major stock market crashes since the beginning of the market.

Major Market Crashes 1900 - Present

Period	% of Loss	Years to Recovery
1901-1903	46%	2 Years
1906-1907	49%	9 Years
1916-1917	40%	2 Years
1919-1921	47%	3 Years
1929-1932	89%	22 Years
1939-1942	40%	3 Years
1973-1974	45%	8 Years
1987-1987	36%	3 Years
2000-2003	32%	6 Years
2007-2008	49%	5 Years
2022-?	18%	??

Average Loss of 47% Every 11 Years!

Turning to some of the most recent crashes, in 1987, the day we now call "Black Monday," the market witnessed a 36% crash in a single day. It took three years to recover from that rut.

In 2002, we had the "dot com crash." Tech stocks lost about

70% and the market lost 32% overall on average. This crash took six years just to break even.

And we can't forget the housing crash that spanned 2007-2008, when the stock market lost an average of 49%. It was five long years before we saw the market recover from those losses.

In the last 20 years, we have spent 11 of those just trying to dig out of a hole. No one can get ahead that way!

Recent headlines have begun to forecast the gloomy future many expect:

- Dow's point drop worst on record[2]
- Dow posts biggest single day drop[3]
- U.S. Inflation Unexpectedly Accelerates to a 40-Year High of 8.6%[4]
- 98% of CEOs Prepping for US recession[5]
- U.S. National Debt Tops $30 Trillion as Borrowing Surged Amid Pandemic[6]

FYI: Forbes reports that the national debt is expected to rise to nearly $89 trillion by 2029.[7]

It's impossible to ignore the impact these issues will have on our economy and stock market. That's why I always advise planning for market fluctuations as a key element of a *No-Stress Retirement* plan. They *will* happen.

Wealth Killer #2: Taxes
The next biggest wealth killer is taxes. And while I can't help you avoid all taxes, I can certainly show you how to lower them.

The 401(k) and IRA and other qualified plans are tax-deferred plans. That means that the money that you contribute goes in pre-tax and grows tax-deferred. You only pay taxes on the money that you take out. You are still paying taxes, just at a later time.

But—and, like before, this is a big "but"—what will the tax rate be when you actually withdraw the money? What if that's 10, 20, or 30 years from now?

What if I told you that federal taxes are near their lowest rates in history? You may not feel that way when you send in your tax check on April 15th, but as the chart on the below illustrates, federal taxes are comparatively low. Regardless of whether you are in the lowest tax or highest bracket, this is the time to consider paying taxes on your nest egg.

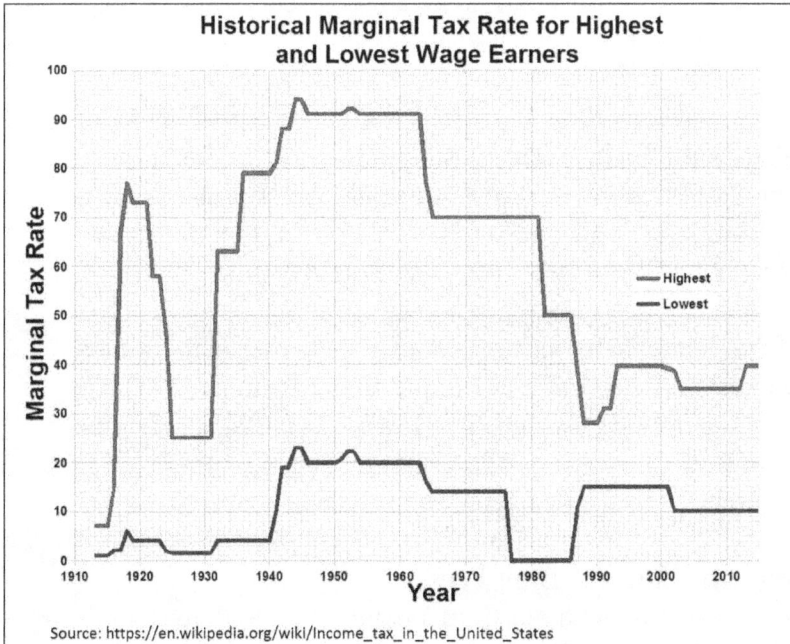

Source: https://en.wikipedia.org/wiki/Income_tax_in_the_United_States

Now let me remind you of a second critical factor: we have witnessed out-of-control government spending for decades, and there is no end in sight. Inflation is screaming. The deficit is at an all-time high and rising. Military spending is at an all-time high. We are funding yet another war. Will taxes go up? It is my strong belief that they will, and probably by a huge amount.

You might be saying to yourself that you have been told it's better to pay taxes later while in retirement because you will be in a lower tax bracket. That would be true if a "lower tax bracket in retirement" is achievable. But, as I suggested earlier, that lower tax bracket can be difficult to hit if your two biggest tax deductions are gone, namely mortgage interest and child tax credits. If you are an empty-nester and your house is paid for, let me be the first to congratulate you. Job well done! But with that congratulations may come an official welcome letter to a higher tax bracket. It's not a bad place to be—as long as you planned for it.

If you have saved and invested well, your retirement assets, along with Social Security, should provide retirement income similar to that in your working years, which means your tax bracket won't change. And that, of course, should be your goal. Remember, retirement may cost more than you think.

If you agree that your tax cost may be higher in the future, what should you do? The simple answer is to pay the taxes now—before they go up. There are two strategies to do just that: Roth conversions and using the tax-free benefits of life insurance. Both are covered in upcoming chapters.

Wealth Killer #3: High Fees

That leaves us with our third wealth killer, high fees. Let's say you pay a measly 1.19% toward the published mutual fund fees. That doesn't sound bad, right? Where else can you get a relatively diverse investment for just 1.19% in fees?

The problem is there are typically far more fees than the published (aka "disclosed") fees. I like to call them the "silent killers" because you never hear about the true costs. According to Forbes, hidden costs can tack on an additional 1.44% on the average.[8] Tax inefficiencies cost you another 1.1% on average. And then we get to "sneaky behavior." Add another 2.49% on average for these virtually undetectable, mutual fund hidden fees, and you've pretty much eliminated the chance of making much money in mutual funds.

How much can these fees add up? Let's take a look at the numbers for a 25-year-old investor:
- Has $25,000 balance in a retirement fund
- Contributes $10,000 a year
- Earns an average of 7% annually in the retirement fund

Paying just 1% in fees would cost more than $590,000 in sacrificed returns over 40 years of saving. Multiply that by the true cost of mutual funds, and you should be frightened! Low-fee and no-fee programs are the key to keeping more of your money. Yes, there are such things!

Wealth Killer #4: Inflation
There's an elephant in the room that we haven't considered yet: inflation. And that's something that we need to think about now more than ever.

From 1929 to 2022, inflation ranged from -10.3% to a high of 18.1%. The average comes to 3.17%. If we use that average, what would your $100 be worth in 20 years? $53.57! In other words, if we use history as any sort of guide, the price of living will nearly double every 20 years. This means your retirement income will need nearly double just to keep up. Just to stay even.

But we're not in Kansas anymore, Dorothy. As I am pounding away at my keyboard on this book, reported inflation is just over 9%! Many believe that the true number is actually much higher, but it's intentionally not being accurately reported. Did eggs only go up 9%? Gas? Beef? I can't think of anything that only went up 9%. If inflation keeps up at present levels, the cost of living will double in just eight years. Can you say the same about your retirement account and your income?

With that in mind, how do you make sure you don't run out of money in retirement? How can you ensure you are not trying to make ends meet by working as a Walmart greeter at the ripe age of 85?

Unfortunately, plenty of people enter retirement under the assumptions that we all make: we saved, we did our time, now we are entitled to enjoy life. Problematically, "enjoying life" becomes a lot more expensive when we least expected it. If our account also plummeted because of stock market fluctuations, then we are facing a nightmare. We are running out of money.

This is what happened to my parents, and it happens to far too many people. Lots of retirees have a few great retirement years, spending their retirement money and having fun. But then one day, they check their accounts and do some math. They realize they are running out of money because they spent too much, because things cost far more than they ever expected or they lost money in the stock market. As a result, they end up entering a new phase: pinching pennies for the rest of their retirement.

This is the stage of panic that I hope every client of mine can avoid. It's great to have a job if you *want* to work in retirement, but it's quite another thing to **have** to work in retirement.

Fortunately, there is a solution. There's something I call the *"Fill-the-Gap Income Plan"* that ensures your expenses are met for the rest of your life. You can enjoy the retirement that you planned, and saved for, all those years. I detail this solution in the next chapter, *Why Fill-the-Gap Income Planning Is Vital*.

Section 1

Fill-the-Gap Income Plan

Why Fill-the-Gap Income Planning is Vital

The most crucial element of a *No-Stress Retirement* plan is not worrying about having the money to pay your bills and losing your nest egg to market crashes. So, with all the details that I covered in previous chapters, here's one of the most important features on the retirement roadmap: *Fill-the-Gap Income Planning*.

Some of the following guidance is geared toward working families, but it certainly applies to those in retirement as well. Given the limited ability to increase income while in retirement, the planning suggestions are of ever-increasing importance when you are no longer earning an income.

Fill-the-Gap Income Planning will do two things for you:

1) offer a guide to understand what income you will need in retirement and how it may change over time.

2) provides income to cover your expenses

As I said earlier, it's great to have a job in retirement if you want to work. But it's quite another to have to work in retirement. So, let's *"Fill the Gap"* by talking about budgeting. Trust me, creating an honest budget, and sticking with it, may be the most important advice you will read in this book.

But what exactly is budgeting? Simply put, it's a proactive approach to organizing your finances. Budgeting ensures you're not spending more than you're making, allowing you to plan for short- and long-term expenses. It may not be easy when you first try it, but it allows you, and people with all types of income and expenses, to keep finances in order.

Below I give you a five-step process that helps you figure out a true budget for you and your household. The process starts with itemizing your monthly expenses that will fulfill your retirement dreams. We typically need to guesstimate increased medical costs, visits to the kids and grandkids, new cars, maybe a boat, an RV, or a world cruise. The important exercise is to write down the costs and anticipated future expenses and total them on paper.

Next, you need to figure out your income. Total up your pension—if you are so lucky to have one—as well as rental income, Social Security, and dividends from your investments and any other income.

This is the only way to figure out if you have a "Gap." If you do, that must be filled. And when I say "filled," it needs to be filled for a lifetime. Otherwise, you may have to reduce your lifestyle or get a job in retirement.

I believe these three golden rules of budgeting will never change:
- Golden Rule #1: Don't spend more than your income.
- Golden Rule #2: Always plan for the future.
- Golden Rule #3: Make your money grow.

And I like to follow those Golden Rules with a basic five-step plan:

Step #1
Calculate your net income. The foundation of an effective

budget will always be a realistic look at your income, and it's best to base this on your after-tax income. If you get a regular paycheck, the amount you receive is probably it. But on top of this, you have automatic deductions for a 401(k), savings, and health and life insurance. Add those back in to give yourself a true picture of your savings and expenditures. If you have other types of income, subtract anything that reduces it, such as taxes and business expenses. If your income is commission-based, then use a conservative estimate.

If you are receiving Social Security, the percentage of your benefit that is taxed is dependent on the amount of earned income that you have. That will change as your income fluctuates, so that is a consideration as well when determining your after-tax benefit amount.

Step #2
Calculate your expenses and be realistic about them. Track where your money went and where it is going—every dime if you must. Categorize these into fixed and variables costs, and define them under subjects such as Home, Utilities, Auto, Entertainment, Savings, etc. I find the most accurate method is to review all your past expenditures and anticipate they will be higher.

This is a great December project, by the way. That's when the calendar year winds down and you're figuring out an annual budget as a New Year's resolution.

Add in future expenses, such as vacations, new cars, a boat or RV, etc. Any upcoming, large expense should be accounted for as part of your total.

Step #3
Calculate the difference. This will be your "Gap." I hope this will be a positive number but if it isn't, you have a problem

that needs to be solved! A negative balance will take away from your future and limit your retirement potential.

If you have a negative Gap, you will need to reassess both Step #1 and Step #2. You will have no other option. During your retirement years, if you are on a fixed income, a negative Gap can limit your dreams. If you are younger, maybe a millennial, and have a negative Gap, you will face a very challenging future. Remember, you cannot predict the future, but you can do your best to plan for it.

Step #4

Determine what to do with the difference and take action. This is not for the faint of heart. With a negative Gap, you will need to revisit every expense and cut out the fat. If your Gap is still negative, you will need add income with another job or a guaranteed income plan through your investments. This is where a financial professional comes in.

If your Gap is positive, you can create savings. Again, this is where a financial professional can be of great help. Even if your positive Gap is small, you can do better than just putting it in a savings account, a CD, or risking it in the stock market. A professional can show you options to grow your account without risk.

Step #5

This sounds simple, but often is not: make reviewing these steps a habit—a daily habit, a monthly habit, and an annual habit. This final step is sometimes the most difficult, but it is necessary. Forming a financial habit will change your family's self-confidence and your kids' and grandkids' future. You may falter from time to time, and fall off the financial planning wagon, but if you do, you will need to pick yourself right back up or you will be denying your best retirement dreams.

Obviously, there are no guarantees with these five steps, but they should give you a foundation to financial security.

I have found that one of the most common percentage-based budgets is something called the 50/30/20 rule. The idea is to divide your income into three categories, spending 50% on fixed and recurring needs, 30% on what you want or might need, and 20% on savings for your future. This is not for everyone, but it does offer a place to start.

The Pew Research Center defines the middle class as households that earn between two-thirds and double the median U.S. household income, which was $65,000 in 2021, according to the U.S. Census Bureau. Using Pew's yardstick, middle class income should be somewhere between $43,350 and $130,000 per year. Most of you reading these words will fall into this category. Even if you have a higher income, the five steps I've outlined will be useful.

Simply put, if your annual income is $100,000, with the 50/30/20 rule, as much as $20,000 of your income should be saved or invested. A good budget will outline how this can be done.

Now think about this. Wouldn't it be nice if you had a never-ending supply of money and never had to worry about any of this budgeting stuff? No worries about planning. No worries about filling in the Gap. Living a totally carefree life. Well, in reality, even for the wealthy, this just isn't the case.

Everyone, no matter their station in life, will benefit by following a well-planned budget. Budgets allow you to determine, in advance, whether you will have enough money to do what you want to in retirement. It's that simple.

In today's digital world, choosing a way to budget can involve easily available downloaded software. I will list seven that are available on the Internet. They are in no particular order, and I make no specific recommendations as to which one will fit your needs. I suggest you do your own research and check out each of them to see which would work best for you:

You Need a Budget or YNAB—This is a flexible way to meet your needs.

- **Mint**—This app is an all-around good fit for most investors.
- **Goodbudget**—This app is good for those who prefer a hands-on approach.
- **EveryDollar**—This one provides a simple zero-based budgeting platform.
- **Personal Capital**—This app is good for tracking wealth and investments.
- **PocketGuard**—This provides a simplified budgeting concept.
- **Honeydue**—This is great when two people want to share in a budget.

These apps, or even just an Excel spread sheet, can be useful ways to begin budgeting.

I also recommend that you automate your savings as much as possible. This allows money you've allocated for your retirement to be deposited with minimal effort on your part. I also recommend an accountability partner or an online support group that can hold you accountable for the choices you've made.

As I said earlier, this needs to become a habit. Your income, expenses, and priorities will change over time, but the constant should always be a budget. Here are some budgeting tips that might help.

- Evaluate your spending. Study where you can cut back and become more efficient.

- Track your small expenditures. Every single cost adds up. They may be nickel-and-dime expenses, but they could make a difference on the bottom line.

- Set goals and deadlines, and then share them. It's good when someone reminds you why you are following a budget.

- Always look for increased income opportunities. We have witnessed some record unemployment over the past year. How can your talents earn more?

- Since the pandemic hit, a lot of people have started small. Perhaps put aside just 2% or 3% per month, then make it grow.

- Divvy up budgeting responsibilities to other family members. Share the load so you're not the only one trying to save a buck.

- Be efficient with your utilities. Put your heating and cooling on a day or night cycle. This could save a lot, especially when fuel prices have risen.

- If you enjoy grocery shopping, take charge in reducing your food costs. Plan grocery lists and meals around sales and coupons, buy storable items in bulk, and buy fresh produce when in season.

I also advise you to make room for splurges. Even when you adhere to the 50/30/20 rule, there will be a need for rewards. When you or your family have reached some planned milestones, you all deserve a celebration. This is a great way to teach your family that living on a budget doesn't mean the elimination of all benefits. As I have said to many investors experiencing a negative gap: moderation is the key to budgeting and saving.

Finally, I would like to emphasize the importance of coordinating and collaborating with all the members of your household. Discuss your goals with your kids and encourage them to take some responsibility. They all need to be involved in filling the Gap as they will all benefit from a great budget plan. After all, it is a family budget.

5   Fill-the-Gap with Guaranteed Income

The most crucial element of a *No-Stress Retirement* plan is not worrying about having the money to pay your bills and losing your nest egg to market crashes. You need not just income, but guaranteed income, and you need protection from market downfalls.

You may remember this from an earlier chapter, but it's worth repeating: University of Wisconsin-Milwaukee's Professor Bender observed In the *Wall Street Journal* article "The Secret to a Happier Retirement," retirees who receive traditional company pensions are happier than those who have to rely solely on the savings they have amassed in 401(k) and similar retirement savings plans. Understandably, seniors like the sense of security that comes with guaranteed, predictable income.[1]

I will continue by adding this quote which was previously not included: "If you don't have a traditional pension, you could buy yourself a comparable stream of income…"

Nothing lets you sleep as well at night as having guaranteed income for the rest of your life. You can accomplish that with something called "interest contracts."

The goals of the interest contract are to:
    1) participate in the upside of the market
    2) protect your principle from market crashes

Both are vital.

With an interest contract, your money is not invested in the stock market, but it allows you to participate in the upside of the stock market while eliminating market risk. You profit from the gains of the market, but when the market crashes, you won't lose a penny due to market losses.

It may seem too good to be true, but it's not. It's real. It works.

Here's how it's done: In its simplest terms, the interest contract will purchase guaranteed interest bonds. Since bonds don't pay a lot, the interest from the bonds is used as a "multiplier" by purchasing exchange-traded options funds that track indexes. They only use the interest that you earned, not your principal, so your principle is fully protected at all times!

An option allows you (or more specifically gives you the "option") to purchase indexes in the future at a guaranteed price, but it does not require you to make the purchase. You only do so if the value goes up.

When the market goes up, it cannot buy all of the gains. It can only buy a portion of the gains. So, in the following examples, the options will buy 80% of the gains. Even though you don't realize the full gains of the market, eliminating the losses more than makes up for it!

If the index value goes up, you earn profits and they are added to your principle. You have just participated in the upside of the market!

If the index does not increase or crashes, you do not earn interest, and you only lose the money that you used to purchase the options, which came from your bond interest, not your principle. You have just protected your principle from market crashes! While it might sound complicated, you need not worry. The process is all done for you automatically, inside the interest contract, and the results can be impressive!

Let's look at how this can play out in this next chart:

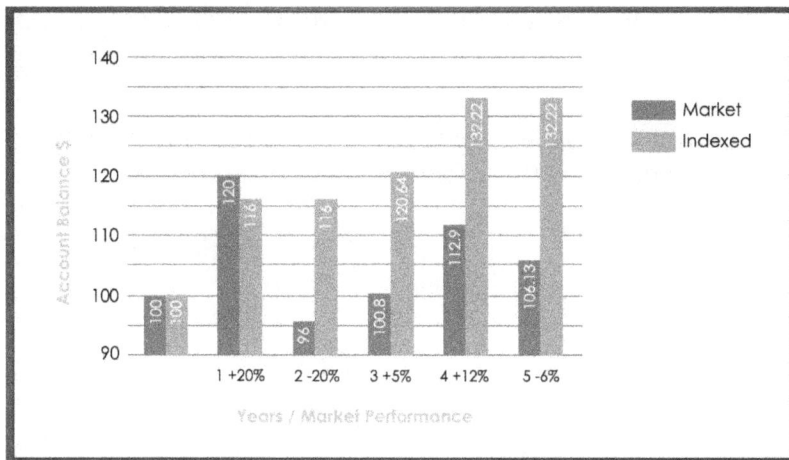

Here the list of events for the stock market indicated in dark gray:

- Year 1) Starting with $100, the market increases 20% and our stock market balance increases to $120

- Year 2) There is a 20% correction, and our balance drops to $96

- Year 3) The market increased 5%, and our balance increases to $100.80

- Year 4) The market increase is 12%, which increases our balance to $112.90

- Year 5) A drop of 6% in the market drops us to $106.13

The indexed performance is in light gray and here are the comparative results:

- Year 1) The market goes up 20% and our $100 starting balance increases to $116, by capturing 80% of the market gain

- Year 2) The market drops year 2 by $20%. We do not lose any money and the balance remains at $116

- Year 3) The market increases 5%. Our portion increases 4%, and our balance increases to $120.64

- Year 4) We gain 9.6% of the market's 12% increase. Our balance increases to $132.22

- Year 5) There is no gain due to the market loss, but we have no losses. Our account remains at $132.22

We end up with $132.22 indexed versus $106.13 in the market. Wow!

Okay, now for some real-life numbers. The following chart tracks the performance of $400,000 starting in 2001 and running through 2020, both invested in the S&P (bottom) and in an indexed interest contract (top). In this example, the indexed performance is capped at 12.5%, (meaning that you won't earn more than 12.5% interest in that year, even if the stock market does better.) There are contract options that do have not caps, but even with the cap, the indexed interest contract far outperformed the S&P.

Growth of Funds with Indexing - Total Deposits: $400,000

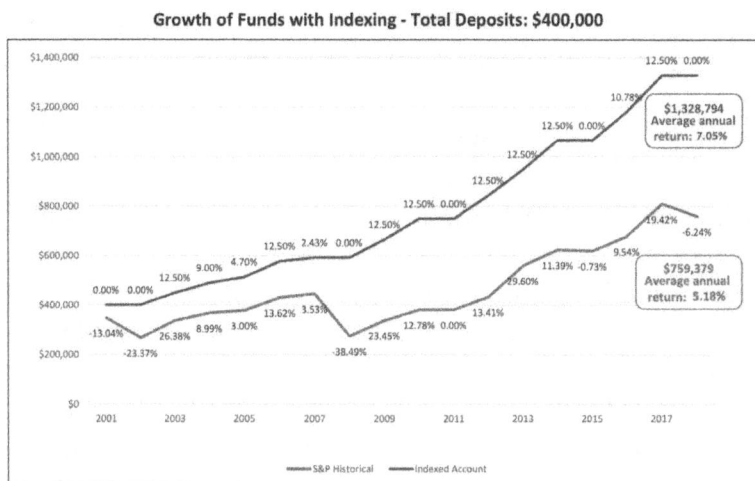

Market returns assume S&P 500 Annual Returns Years 2001-2018, excluding dividends.

Indexed fund values do not include any costs.

Hypothetical example is for illustrative purposes only. This is not a prediction or guarantee of actual results, which will vary from those described.

D. Scott Kozlik does not provide tax, legal or accounting advice, nor is it designed - nor intended - to be applied to any person's individual circumstances. This material has been prepared for information purposes only, and is not intended to provide, and should not be relied on for, tax, legal or accounting advice. You should consult your own qualified tax, legal and accounting advisors before engaging in any transaction.

The S&P performed at 5.18% and totaled $759,379.

The indexed interest contract performed at 7.05% and totaled $1,328,794. It beat the S&P because it doesn't take losses. Enough said!

There's another added benefit to these interest contracts. They can provide a lifetime of guaranteed income for both spouses.

The market protection and lifetime income from the indexed income contract is the basis for our *Fill-the-Gap Income Plan*.

The plan that I created for Betty and Anthony is a great example of this concept. They called me when Anthony was 61. His long-time goal was to retire at 62—the age at which he can start drawing Social Security. Unfortunately, they saw their plan dissolve away before their eyes with the drop in the stock market.

He planned on using his IRA as income in retirement. He knew that while he could afford to retire at 62, they were concerned that his income wouldn't last if the stock market continued to drop or dropped again in the future.

Their anxieties were well-founded. I reviewed the history of the stock market with them and told them that not only could the stock market continue to drop, they may see several more market crashes in their future. The expressions on their faces turned to dread.

We rolled up our sleeves and went to work. I gave them a homework assignment and set up a time for our next meeting. Their job before then was to list their expenses and come up with a monthly budget. They were to also list any major purchases that they planned to make in retirement. Lastly, I asked them to set up an account on ssa.gov and find out what their primary insurance amounts would be at age 62, which would serve as their income cornerstone on which we would build our income plan.

At meeting number two, we compared their expenses and anticipated future income requirements with their Social Security incomes. We determined that Betty and Anthony needed an additional $60,000 annually. Here's the crux: the income needed to be there each and every year, guaranteed.

The solution was simple. The issues would be solved with the interest contract I just described; the kind that is tied to an index that would give them stock-market like gains but would prevent them from losing any money. That would protect them from risk. We took about half of their nest egg and placed it into an income-producing interest contract. This way market crashes would not destroy their balance, and they would receive guaranteed income each month.

With the interest contract, their money was not in the stock market, but their interest credit grew with the stock market. Each year that the stock market increased, their interest would increase; but even if the market remained static, or worse yet, crashed, their account balance would not drop. That solved their lifetime income needs.

Next, we took a portion of their remaining savings and put it into an interest contract designed for maximum growth. This protected the rest of their nest egg from market crashes and provided impressive earnings with no stock market downside.

Result: Their "Gap" was filled and their remaining money grew without stock market risk. They could fulfill their retirement plans and dreams, travel, spoil their grandchildren, and still rest assured their income and savings will be there when they needed it. They were "sleep insured" to the max!

That, my friends, is *Fill-the-Gap Income Planning*.

Guaranteed Interest Contracts

If you are the type of investor that is risk-adverse, and you don't like how an indexing works but still wants competitive returns, a guaranteed interest contract may be right up your alley.

So, what is a guaranteed interest contract? Think of it as CD on steroids. What I mean is that they have the safety and guarantees of a CD, but typically pay a higher interest rate. You are paid a fixed rate, no ifs, ands, or buts, for a specific period of time, typically, one to seven years. Once the contract starts, your interest is locked in for the term you chose. The starting interest rates constantly change, but as I type this chapter, they are hovering in the low 5% range.

Now before you scoff at 5% and skip to the next chapter, there are a couple things to consider:

> 1) When you add in market crashes, the long-term performance of the stock market is just over 5.5%. Sure, we have had lots of great years with double-digit performance, but add in the crashes, and we are looking at just over a 5.5% average.

> 2) That doesn't mean you will earn 5.5% each year in the market, that's the long-term average, which includes highs and crashes. If you need money and the market is down 47%—which is the average major crash over the

life of the market—will your money be there? When your balance is cut in half, will your account be able to sustain your withdrawal needs for living expenses? Also, keep in mind that if you pass during a market downfall, you heirs may get much less.

Take a look at this performance comparison to the stock market:

Year	S&P Performance	S&P Account Balance	4% Guaranteed Interest Contract Account Balance
2000	(-10.14)	$89,860	$104,000
2001	(-13.04)	$78,142	$108,160
2002	(-23.37)	$59,880	$112,486
2003	26.38	$76,676	$116,985
2004	8.99	$82,480	$121,665
2005	3.00	$84,954	$126,531
2006	13.62	$96,525	$131,593
2007	3.53	$99,932	$136,856
2008	(-38.49)	$61,468	$142,331
2009	23.44	$75,877	$148,024
2010	12.80	$85,589	$153,945
2011	0.00	$85,589	$160,103
2012	13.41	$97,066	$166,507
2013	30.00	$126,186	$173,167
2014	11.40	$140,571	$180,094
2014	(-0.7)	$139,588	$187,298
2016	9.54	$152,905	$194,790
2017	19.40	$182,568	$202,581
2018	(-6.59)	$170,537	$210,684
2019	29.00	$219,992	$219,112

The left side of the chart shows a list of the stock market returns from 2000 to 2019. Starting with a $100,000 investment, you ended up at $219,000 over the 20 years.

On the right are the comparative earnings with a 4% guaranteed interest contract. After 20 years, you end up with just about the identical earnings, $219,000.

That shows that a 4% interest contract matched the performance of the stock market from 2000 to 2019, but, and this is yet another big "but," **for 19 out of 20 years, the 4% contract outperformed the stock market, and outperformed it significantly.**

In 2003, we have $75,000 in the market versus $116,000 in the 4% interest contract.

In 2008 we have $61,000 in the market versus $142,000 in the 4% interest contract.

In 2013 we have $126,000 in the market versus $173,000 in the 4% interest contract.

You get the picture.

If you wanted to take out money in any of those 19 years, you would have had far more money in the 4% guaranteed interest contract than if your money was in the stock market. And (this is another big one), when future crashes happen, not only will you not lose a penny with the 4% guaranteed interested contract, but you will also still get your 4% interest.

Slow and steady can win the race. Guaranteed interest contracts can be an important element of a *No-Stress Retirement* plan.

Section II

Traditional Retirement Strategies
and
How to Make the Most of Them

7 The Fallacy of Pre-Tax Investing

There's a lot of advice out there about how to maximize your retirement savings. Unfortunately, a lot of it doesn't get you to where you need to be when you retire. If you listen to what the "experts" say, you will spend a lot of time worrying. Worry equals stress, and that is what we don't wish for anyone when they retire.

Unfortunately, it has been driven into our heads that the best way to save for retirement is to use qualified plans that allow us to contribute pre-tax, grow our account tax-deferred, and only pay taxes when money is withdrawn during retirement. We are talking 401(k)s, IRAs, 403(b)s, 457s and TSPs. The numbers look inviting.

Your two choices are to invest $10,000 without paying tax on it, or pay tax on the $10,000, and only invest $7,500 (assuming 25% tax) in a tax-free account such as a Roth IRA. While the first choice will appear to grow to a larger amount, in reality, there is no advantage.

With the first choice, there is an assumption that the tax rate won't increase 10, 20 or 30 years from now. Color me doubtful, highly doubtful, but even if we assume taxes won't rise by some miracle upon miracle, you will still be paying taxes on the $10,000 plus earnings.

Would you rather pay tax on the seed or on the crop?

The fact is, it *doesn't* matter. Take a look at this chart:

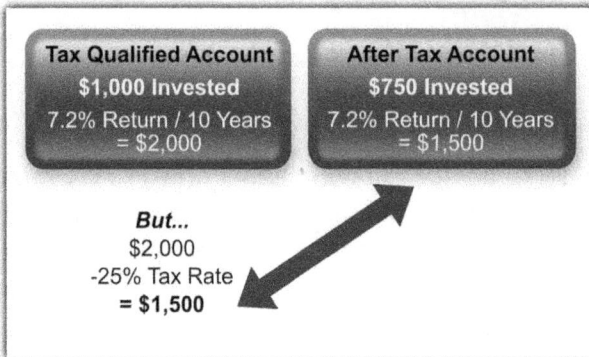

Tax Qualified Account	After Tax Account
$1,000 Invested	$750 Invested
7.2% Return / 10 Years = $2,000	7.2% Return / 10 Years = $1,500

But...
$2,000
-25% Tax Rate
= $1,500

With the first choice, if you invest $1,000 pre-tax for 10 years, and earn 7.2% on your money, it will yield $2,000. But you will need to pay tax on the $2,000. Assuming a 25% tax rate, you end up with $1,500.

With the second choice, if you invest $1,000 after-tax, which is $750 with a 25% tax, and earn 7.2% on your money, you will end up with $1,500.

The result in the end is **exactly the same**.

The advantage is none, nada, zero. But that is only if the tax rates stay exactly as they are now. What if (or more to the point when) taxes go up in the future, you will pay the lower rate if you pay the taxes now.

Americans have been fleeced, manipulated, bamboozled, and brainwashed into thinking that pre-tax investing in qualified plans is the best way to save.

Why? Look at who is giving the advice:

- Uncle Sam, who taxes withdrawals from qualified plans at the highest tax bracket.

- Wall Street, who charges qualified plans their highest fees.

Coincidence?

8 Benefits of Roth Conversions

Roth Conversions have been a hot topic lately and for good reason. They can potentially save you quite a bit of taxes in the long run.

I am going to show you how a Roth Conversion saved one family $213,000; but before I do, I want to give you a little background.

Traditional IRAs and Roth IRAs are qualified plans, meaning they qualify for special tax treatment. The main difference between the two are the tax rules that apply to each.

With Traditional IRAs, the money that you contribute goes in pretax, meaning you don't pay taxes on the money deposited in the plan. The account grows tax deferred, so you pay taxes later, when you take withdrawals in retirement. Even if you don't want income from the IRA, you must take Required Minimum Distributions, also known as RMDs, starting at age 73. And additionally, your heirs will pay taxes when they inherit the account.

The Roth IRA taxation is quite different. You pay taxes on the money that goes into Roth IRA, but the money that has been in your account for at least five years can then be withdrawn tax-free after age 59-1/2. There are no required minimum distributions and Roths are tax-free to the next generation as well as an inheritance.

Now, let's take a look at two scenarios. Scenario #1 is that you use your IRA for income in retirement, and scenario #2 is that your IRA will be passed on to the next generation.

Diane and Paul are in the second scenario. They want to leave their IRA to the kids. They just retired and are doing well financially. They have enough income, annuities, and investments to have a comfortable retirement. They don't need to draw from their IRA, so it will go to their kids with some extra money to spoil their grandchildren.

I am going to show you a comparison on how leaving their money in their IRA would work out tax-wise, compared to if it was converted to a Roth. In this case Diane and Paul are 66 years old and their tax rate is 25%.

Traditional IRA Taxation

Diane and Paul - 66-years-old
$500,000, 5% growth, living to age 90, 25% tax

RMDs to age 90

Total taxes on RMD at withdrawals	$158,235
Taxes on growth of reallocated assets	$69,976
Taxes paid by heirs on remaining value	$110,294
Total Taxes Paid	$338,505

Even though their traditional IRA is meant for an inheritance for their kids, Minimum Required Distributions are required starting at age 73. With their $500,000 account, they will pay a cumulative $158,000 in taxes on their RMDs through age 90.

Since they don't need the money from the RMD themselves, they will reinvest the RMD withdrawals, and will pay $69,000 of taxes on the growth.

When their children get their inheritance, they will have to pay $110,000 in tax. In total, Diane and Paul and their children, will pay over $338,000 in taxes.

Now, let's look at the same situation if they converted to a Roth IRA:

Power of Roth Conversion

Diane and Paul - 66-years-old
$500,000, 5% growth, living to age 90, 25% tax

NO RMDs!!

Total taxes on ROTH Conversion	$125,000
Taxes on growth of reallocated assets	$0
Taxes paid by heirs on remaining value	$0
Total Taxes Paid	$125,000

$500,000 converts to a Roth, and they will pay taxes of $125,000 in income taxes when they convert.

There are no taxes on the growth and no taxes upon inheritance. Their total tax is just $125,000. Their children will receive over $213,000 more if the IRA is converted to a Roth IRA.

That's what I call great tax planning!

Now the other scenario is keeping the IRA and taking withdrawals for retirement income. The big question is the tax rate. As discussed earlier, most of us think that the tax rate will go up in the future and that's hard to argue against. I tend to support any plan that takes advantage of the current tax rate, since I think it is unlikely we will see it again for quite some time.

When converting to a Roth, there are no conversion limits, nor income limits. You can convert all of your account or just a portion.

I do want to add a word of caution. You don't need to convert your entire IRA at one time; you can partially convert it out over several years, which is important because of tax brackets.

When you convert, the amount of Traditional IRA money that you convert to Roth is considered income. **So you need to be careful that the increased income does not push you into a higher tax bracket,** *unless that's your goal.* For this reason, it is important to work with a tax professional to determine how much you can convert each year, without increasing your tax bracket.

Note: I talked about converting your traditional IRA to a Roth, but you can do the same with 401(k)s, 403(b)s, TSPs (Thrift Savings Plans), and other qualified accounts by first rolling them into an IRA, then doing a Roth conversion.

This is a chart of the 2023 US federal tax brackets
Keep in mind that they change often

TAX BRACKETS FOR 2023		
Rate	Single Filer	Married, Filing Jointly
10%	$0 to $11,000	$0 to $22,000
12%	$11,001 to $44,725	$22,001 to $89,450
22%	$44,726 to $95,375	$89,451 to $190,750
24%	$95,376 to $182,100	$190,751 to $364,200
32%	$182,101 to $231,250	$364,201 to $462,500
35%	$231,251 to $578,125	$462,501 to $693,750
37%	$578,126 or more	$693,751 or more

9   Dump Your 401(k) as Soon as Possible

401(k) plans are the cornerstone of most Americans' retirement plans. They were created when Congress passed the Revenue Act of 1978. The Act included a provision—Section 401(k)— that gave employees a tax-free way to defer compensation from wages, bonuses, or stock options. The law went into effect on January 1, 1980, and transformed the concept of retirement plans forevermore. To quote the Beatles, "…some have changed. Some forever, not for better."[8]

The two greatest theoretical benefits of 401(k) plans are that they are "qualified plans" and most employers offer an incentive for employees to save for their retirement by "matching" employee contributions. But are these "benefits" beneficial? Let's explore the concept.

As detailed in the chapter, *The Fallacy of Pre-Tax Investing*, there is no advantage in investing on a pre-tax basis. Worse yet, it may end up costing you more in the end. I encourage you to read the chapter again for additional explanations and details.

That leaves us with benefit number two, employer matching. With most 401(k) plans, employers will match a certain percentage of employee contributions. The contribution amount usually has a limit, and the match has a limit. A generous employer will offer a 100% match, with every dollar an employee contributes being matched by the company. It could cover up to 3%, 5%, or 10% of employee pay, or even more depending on the plan design and limits. The match is **FREE** money!!! That's great! Who in their right mind would turn down free money??? So, why am I saying that it may not really be a benefit?

Let's start with the employers' motivation. Back before 401(k) plans were a thing, employers offered Pension Plans. If you were lucky enough to work for a company that provided them and stayed employed long enough, you would get a payment for the rest of your life after retirement. This was often distributed at a certain percentage of your pay. Highly valued employees were offered what is known as a "Golden Parachute," which meant that if they were employed long enough, they would get 100% of their pay, for life, after retirement. It was a sweet deal. These pension plans were used not only as compensation, but also incentives for employees to stay with the company.

Did you notice what is not included in the old-style pension plans? Employee contributions. Pension plans are paid 100% by the employer. Not a penny was paid by the employees themselves. This is a tremendous difference between the two concepts.

When 401(k)s came into existence, companies jumped at the opportunity to drop their expensive pension plans and transition to the 401(k) where their costs were dramatically reduced. Instead of paying 100% of the cost, they now spent a fraction of the cost. Even the most generous plan offering a 100% match of employee contributions of 15% cost employers a fraction of what it would take to give full income for life after retirement.

At this time, very few corporations continue to offer pension plans. Pension plans are most often only found at government jobs and some unions.

Given the fact that pensions no longer exist for the most part, and 401(k) plans are the only corporate-sponsored options, the company match is free money that we should be grateful for, right? Yes! However, that free money comes at a cost; 401(k)s are very expensive.

In the chapter, Four Greatest Wealth Killers, I talked about the high cost of fees and how just 1% in fees can mean a 28% difference in your retirement account. Now, consider this: the average 401(k) plan charges over 2.2% and hidden fees can dramatically up that to boot!

You can do your own research on "Hidden 401(k) Fees," and you will be flabbergasted by articles from *Forbes, 60 Minutes,* and many more. In a *CNBC* article, the "Father of the 401(k)," Ted Benna, tells *The Journal* with some regret that he "… helped open the door for Wall Street to make even more money than they were already making."[9]

To add insult to injury, depending on your tax bracket, approximately 24% of the money in your 401(k) is not yours. It belongs to Uncle Sam in the form of future taxes. You are paying fees on money that you owe the government. Allow me to repeat . . . You are paying fees on money that you owe the government. Let that sink in for a few minutes.

The next element in the cost of a 401(k) is taxes. Withdrawals from 401(k)s are taxed at the highest tax rate, ordinary income. And, if that was not enough, taxes will most likely be higher when you take the money out years from now in retirement.

Add in the facts that plan guidelines can restrict access to your money, investment options are limited, distribution flexibility is limited, and your account is at risk from market crashes, placing your money in a 401(k) may be more of a financial liability than a benefit.

If you have not heard of these issues before, you might be thinking that I must be crazy, or that I am trying to pull the wool over your eyes. You are thinking this just can't be true. Well, it's not just me.

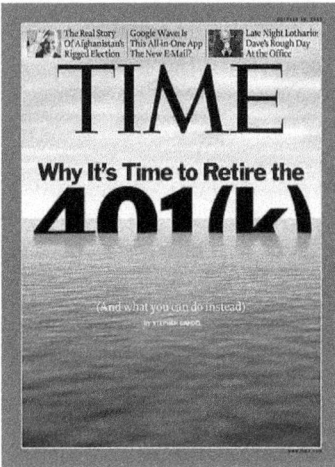

Writing in the October 19, 2009, issue of Time, "Why It's Time to Retire the 401(k)," Stephen Gandel writes that, "The ugly truth though is that the 401(k) is a lousy idea, a financial flop, a rotten repository for our retirement reserves . . ." [10]

The *Fiscal Times* wrote: "The Retirement Revolution that Failed: Why the 401(k) Isn't Working."[11]

In an article entitled "The 401k Scam," *Economic Populist* landed this doozy: "The 401(k) will turn out to be the greatest systemic financial hoax ever perpetrated on an unsuspecting public."[12]

You may be asking yourself: If the 401(k) is so bad, why are we all told that it's the best way to save for retirement? The answer is the old cliché, "Follow the Money."

Your employer pushes the 401(k) because it is an "Employee Benefit" that **you** pay for, and they don't have to shell out for vastly more expensive pensions.

Wall Street pushes the 401(k), because they charge qualified plans the highest fees, and Uncle Sam pushes them because withdrawals from 401(k)s are taxed at the highest tax category.

See a pattern?

So, what do I suggest?

While the costs are expensive, the free employer match makes it worthwhile. Contribute up to the employer match and put the rest of your money in a better place. If you put in 10% and your employer matches up to 5%, reduce your contribution to 5% and put the rest in a lower-cost vehicle.

Secondly, get your money out of the 401(k) as soon as you are able. You can withdraw from your 401(k) when you change jobs or retire. Take your money out as soon as you can. Far too many people I talk with have money in 401(k) years after leaving a job. All of those expensive fees are just money wasted.

Also, a large percentage of plans allow "in-service" withdrawals once the employee turns age 59-1/2. Contact your plan administrator to see if that option is available to you. After you do, continue to contribute to the plan to get the maximum employer match. Withdraw the balance again once the plan allows.

Remember: If you withdraw funds from your 401(k) you will have to pay income tax on the amount taken, but you can "roll over" your 401(k) to an IRA and it will be considered an "nontaxable event." You won't pay a dime in taxes. You will have to pay income tax later when you withdraw from the IRA though.

CHAPTER

10 Social Security;
What You Need to Know

Social Security is the bedrock of many Americans' retirement income. It is a guaranteed, lifetime income and forms the base for the *Fill-the-Gap* planning that I covered earlier. Whether it's your sole source of retirement income or just a portion, it is important to understand your benefits. Tomes have been written about Social Security, but suffice to say, it's just too much information; so I have abridged this chapter to include what you need to know.

A Brief History, Very Brief
President Roosevelt signed the Social Security Act of 1935 into law on August 14, 1935. At the time benefits were to start at age 65. An interesting factoid is that in 1935, the average life expectancy was 66 years, so it was expected at the time that Social Security benefits would last just one year. Yup, you read that right.

In 1935, there were 52,236 Social Security beneficiaries. In 2020, there were 65 million. Given that current life expectancy is much higher, and the population has skyrocketed since inception, the program had to evolve to keep up, and boy has it ever.

Social Security Going Broke?
Given the high financial demands on the program and the ever-persisting news articles proclaiming that Social Security is running out of money, one of the most common questions that I get is, "Will Social Security be available when I retire?"

In a word, yes. The good news is that there was $2.8 trillion in the Social Security trust fund as of the end of 2022. The bad news is that at the going rate, the trust fund is expected to be depleted by 2034. That is, unless changes are made.

Changes can be made in two areas: funding and expenditures. Funding to Social Security is not done by the government, it is done by you, the American workers and by employers through FICA taxes. You will see those deductions on your paystub, and your employer pays an equal portion as well. You are taxed up to a certain level of your income. As of 2023, it's $162,000. They can, and have, changed the taxation level several times. They can and have changed the benefit amounts. They can change the Cost-of-Living Increases; they can change the Full Retirement Age. Basically, they can change just about anything.

Eligibility

Not everyone is eligible for Social Security benefits:

- First off, you have to be a certain age to qualify. Currently, you can start benefits as early as age 62, with reduced benefits.

- You have to have paid FICA taxes for at least ten years (40 quarters). They don't have to be continuous; your working years just have to total ten years. If you have only worked 9.5 years, you will have to get back to work for another six months to qualify.

- Non-working spouses can qualify for a portion of their working spouse's benefits. More on that later.

- Ex-spouses can also qualify for a portion of their ex's benefits as well. More on that later as well.

- There are widow and widower benefits. Yup, more on that coming up.

- Dependent minor children and dependent parents can qualify.

- Those injured may qualify for disability as well, which is a part of Social Security.

- Some government employees and teachers are not eligible, and if that's the case, they do not pay FICA taxes.

When is The Best Age to Start Social Security?
That, my friends, is a question for the ages. It is the most common question that I get about Social Security and the answer is easy: it depends.

Before I broach that subject, let's define a couple of terms:

1) **Full Retirement Age** (FRA) is the age that you get 100% of your Social Security benefits.

2) **Primary Insurance Amount** (PIA) is the benefit amount that you will receive.

Your Full Retirement Age is based on your date of birth as shown in the chart on the next page.

Age for Full Retirement Benefits	
Birth Year	**FRA**
1937 and earlier	65
1938	65 and 2 months
1939	65 and 4 months
1940	65 and 6 months
1941	65 and 8 months
1942	65 and 10 months
1943 – 1954	66
1955	66 and 2 months
1956	66 and 4 months
1957	66 and 6 months
1958	66 and 8 months
1959	66 and 10 months
1960 and later	67

Your Primary Insurance Amount is calculated by your top 35 years' worth of earnings. While you pay into the system with each paycheck with the FICA tax, it is important to understand that you will not necessarily receive back what you put in. There is no "account" in your name with a dollar value attached to it. You are paid benefits for your lifetime. The shorter you live, the less you will receive. Likewise, the longer you live, the more you will get. If you turn on benefits on Monday, and get hit by a truck on Tuesday, you will receive one benefit check, regardless of the tens of thousands you may have paid in FICA taxes over your career. If you live to 100, congrats on numerous levels. You beat the system and Social Security will pay you more than you put in.

At your Full Retirement Age, you will get 100% of your Primary Insurance Amount. You may, however, elect to take your benefits before your FRA, in which case you will get a reduced amount. You can do so starting at age 62. You may also delay turning on your benefits until after your FRA, and you will receive a higher amount. This is called Delayed Retirement Credits (DRC). The chart on the next page indicates the percentage of your PIA that you will receive based on the age that you began receiving benefits.

Less Before – More After
% of PIA   FRA=66

62	63	64	65	**FRA**	67	88	69	70

Delayed Retirement Credits

-25%	-20%	-13.3%	-6.7%	**100%**	+8%	+16%	+24%	+32%

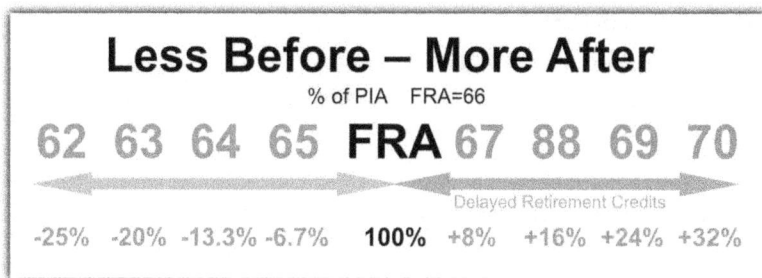

There are a couple of important items to note: The earlier that you take benefits, the lower they will be and the longer you wait, the higher your benefits will be. Keep in mind, once you start your benefits, they will not change other than from cost-of-living increases. As you can see, turning on benefits age 70 increases your benefits each year by 8%, for your lifetime. That's a hefty increase if you can afford to wait. It is important to realize that Delayed Retirement Credits no longer increase after age 70, so never wait longer than age 70 to start receiving your Social Security benefits.

> One client did just that. He came to me at age 71 and he had not taken Social Security yet. When I asked why, he said that he would get more money if he waited until age 72. This mistake cost him dearly. Not only would his benefit not increase after age 70, but he also lost a year of payments and back payments are not possible.

The chart below shows various amounts that you will receive based on the age that you start, using 66 as Full Retirement Age and a PIA of $1980.

62	63	64	65	**66**	67	68	69	70
$1485	$1584	$1716	$1847	$1980	$2138	$2303	$2455	$2613

Benefit Statements

By setting up an account at www.ssa.gov, you can view the earnings from which your benefits are calculated. You will see your wages listed for each year.

You can also see charts that will show your Primary Insurance Amount at Full Retirement Age, and your benefits at different ages.

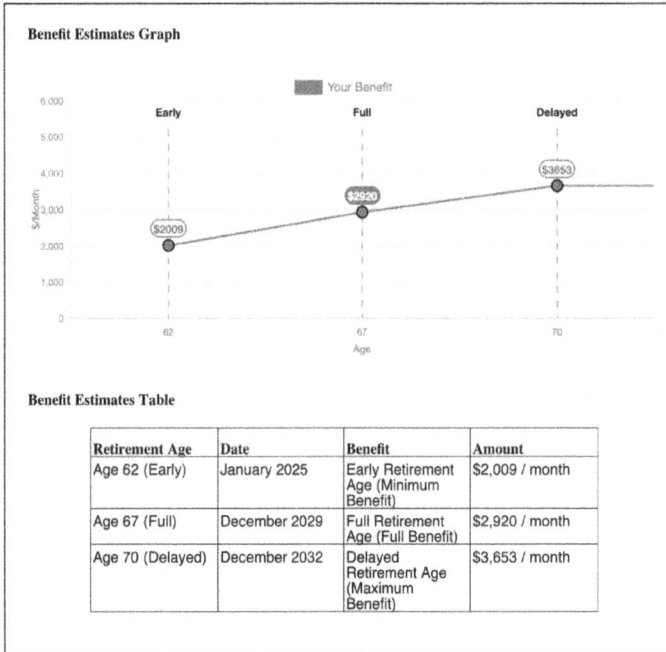

Benefit Estimates Graph

Benefit Estimates Table

Retirement Age	Date	Benefit	Amount
Age 62 (Early)	January 2025	Early Retirement Age (Minimum Benefit)	$2,009 / month
Age 67 (Full)	December 2029	Full Retirement Age (Full Benefit)	$2,920 / month
Age 70 (Delayed)	December 2032	Delayed Retirement Age (Maximum Benefit)	$3,653 / month

Personalized Monthly Retirement Benefit Estimates (Depending on the Age You Start)

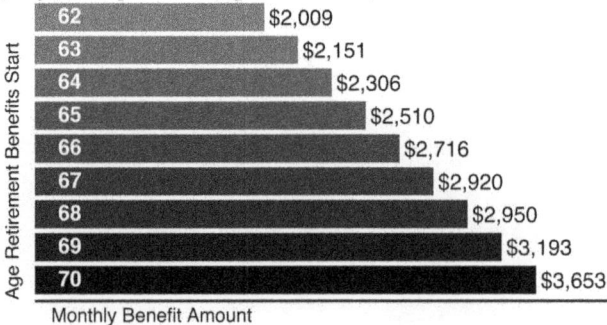

Age Retirement Benefits Start	Monthly Benefit Amount
62	$2,009
63	$2,151
64	$2,306
65	$2,510
66	$2,716
67	$2,920
68	$2,950
69	$3,193
70	$3,653

You should gather this information and have it available for your financial professional to use to create your income plan.

When you are ready to start your benefits, the website is the easiest method. You can also try calling them or stopping into a local office. Good luck with those. My choice is the website.

The Social Security office will never contact you to tell you to turn on your benefits. It's up to you to do that.

Cost of Living Increases
Social Security benefits come with Cost-of-Living increases. They vary year to year, based on inflation. The increase in 2022 was 5.9%, the highest in about 37 years; 2023's increase was an astounding 8.7%!

Are these high increases good news? **NO!** It's terrible news! It means rampant inflation!

When is a benefit increase bad? When your expenses rise higher than your benefit increase!

High Cost of Living increases means that the cost of living has increased, but the true cost of living has increased far higher than the Social Security payments. The highest Cost of Living increase in Social Security in about 40 years is matched by the highest inflation in about 40 years.

The Cost-of-Living Social Security increase for 2023 of 8.7 percent is very close to the reported 9% inflation. However, you know from a previous chapter, I don't believe is true. How much more do you pay for eggs and milk than you did a year ago? Meat? How much more is gas? I bet you now pay much more than 9% than you did a year ago. That goes for just about anything you buy. I can't think of anything that only increased 9% from a year ago.

Here's a kicker: while the Social Security payment increased, so did the cost of Medicare Part B. What the government giveth, the government taketh away.

Spousal Benefits

In the eligibility section, I mentioned that non-working spouses may receive Social Security benefits based on their working spouse. It actually goes a bit deeper than that.

A spouse that is not eligible for Social Security, whether they didn't work enough years, or even if they didn't work at all, may collect half of the qualified spouse's benefits, once the qualified spouse starts their benefits.

Also if a spouse is qualified to collect Social Security, but because of low income, their PIA is low, the spouse may collect half of the qualified spouse's benefits, once the qualified spouse starts collection. You can take whichever benefit is higher.

Which spouse is qualified or low paid, versus which spouse is the one with the high benefit does not matter. It could be the man or women or either side, but let's use John as the qualifying spouse and Mary as the homemaker who never worked as an example, as that is quite a common occurrence.

If John's PIA is $1980 and Mary's is $400, Mary can choose either her own benefit or half of John's. In this case half of John's is $975, making it the obvious choice.

When Should I Take My Social Security Benefits?

Like I said, it depends. Yes, the longer you wait, the more you will receive, but that is not always the smart move. If you don't have enough alternative income to retire and need the Social

Security benefits to retire at 62, by all means take it at 62. If you want the added income to travel, spoil the grandkids, pay for their college, etc., take it.

If you have other income or are still working, and don't need it, you may want to hold off on collecting because each year that you wait after FRA, your benefit increases by 8% each year. But what if you wait until 70, then pass at age 71? You will only receive one year of benefits. Which leads me to my next subject: maximization.

Social Security Maximization
Sounds sexy, huh? Everyone loves maximization. Many advisors offer a service to calculate when each spouse should take Social Security based on your income, age, expenses, and primary insurance amount in order to maximize the lifetime total. Some advisors charge for the service, some offer it as give-away to get you to do business with them, and you can even find software online to do it.

The concept is all based on your age, income, needs, and the law of averages. The calculations are all based on average life expectancies. But are you average? By definition, half will live longer than average, half will live less. The only true way to calculate your maximum benefit is to know exactly what age you are going to pass. Since we don't, any Social Security Maximization plan is just a guess. While your genealogy will give you a hint, your parents may have lived to their 90s and their great genes may have been passed to you, or not. Or you get hit by a fast-moving train at age 63.

Getting a Maximization report is good, but keep in mind, it's just a guess. There is no "right time" to turn on Social Security that works for everyone. It depends.

Earnings Test

If you take Social Security before your Full Retirement Age (FRA) and are still working, either full or part-time, your benefits will be subject to the Annual Earnings Test. If your earnings pass a certain earnings amount, your Social Security benefits will be reduced.

If you take Social Security and are younger than your FRA, the Earnings Test limit for 2023 is $21,240. If you earn more than $21,240, your Social Security will be reduced by $1 for every $2 over the limit. You will be hit with what amounts to a 50% penalty.

The year that you reach FRA, the 2023 limit is $56,520. If you earn more than $56,520, your Social Security will be reduced by $1 for every $3 over the limit. You will be hit with what amounts to a 33% penalty.

That changes once you reach the month of your FRA. At that point, there are no income limits. Keep in mind that the limits do change, so if you are working while taking Social Security before your FRA, make sure you check the limits.

Survivor Benefits

When one spouse passes the remaining spouse can collect their own benefit, or the deceased spouse's benefit, whichever is higher. Delayed Retirement Credits of the deceased spouse will be paid to the remaining spouse.

In order to qualify, the remaining spouse must be at least age 60, or age 50 if disabled. If the deceased spouse was collecting Social Security at the time of death, the surviving spouse may receive that benefit amount.

If the deceased spouse was not collecting Social Security at the time of death, the surviving spouse may elect to collect the deceased spouse's benefit, or wait and allow it to increase with the Delayed Retirement Credits.

Divorced Spouses

Divorced spouses can file for Social Security on the ex-spouse as long as they were married for at least ten years, have been divorced for at least two years, and have not remarried before age 60.

There is no limit to the number of ex-spouses that can collect as long as they meet the requirements. The good news is that unlike alimony, the ex-spouse benefits do not reduce the other spouse's benefits.

Social Security Taxation

The benefits paid to you from Social Security are tax preferred. What I mean by that is not all of the benefits are taxed. The percentage of your Social Security benefits that are federally taxed is based on the amount of your income.

The calculation starts with what is called Provisional Income.

Provisional Income is:

> Adjusted Gross Income
> + Tax exempt income (not Roth IRA or Index Universal Life Insurance income)
> + Excluding foreign income
> + 50% of your Social Security Benefit
> _____
> = Provisional Income

Your provisional income amount is what is used to determine what percentage of your Social Security is federally taxed, and you can see that in the following chart:

% Taxed	File - Single	File - Married
0%	Less than $25,000	Less than $32,000
50%	$25,000 to $34,000	$32,000 to $44,000
85%	$34,000+	$44,000+

Earning $25k single or $32k married, or less, means none of your Social Security will be taxed.

If you file married and earn $32,000 to $44,000, 50% of your Social Security benefits will be taxed federally.

85% of your Social Security will be taxed if you earn $34k single or $44k married.

Leave it to the government to take a simple concept and make it complicated.

Social Security is taxed as ordinary income. Also, to add insult to injury, some states also tax Social Security. To date, the list includes: CO, CT, KS, MI, MO, MT, NE, ND, RI, VT and WV.

Reducing Social Security Taxes
I am absolutely amazed and appalled that a benefit that we paid for with our hard-earned wages is to be portioned back to us and taxed! But that's the world we live in, and we can't change that. However, we can change how much we are taxed.

Here are a few tax reduction options:

Your IRA withdrawals are included in the provisional income calculation. If, by chance, you have a big expense planned upon retirement, like a world cruise, a new car, a RV, etc. and you plan to pay for is with a withdrawal from your IRA, take that money out before turning on Social Security so it won't show up in the income calculation.

Withdrawals from Roth IRAs are non-taxable and thus not included as income in the Provisional Income calculations. Doing a Roth Conversion would not only allow you to pay taxes now, before they increase and give your heirs tax-free money, it also can lower the percentage of your Social Security that is taxed. If all of your income comes from a Roth, you won't pay any income tax, not even on your Social Security.

The same holds true for loans from a type of life insurance policy that I will talk about in the next section. These policy loans are tax-free and won't count toward Social Security taxation. These policy loans are actually an often unknown and underutilized benefit of life insurance. If that piques your curiosity and makes you want to keep reading, then I've done my job.

11 Avoiding IRA Mistakes

Approximately 28% of American households have an IRA account. Unfortunately, there are several mistakes that can cost you money and/or have irreversible repercussions. I am going to cover the four most common so you can hopefully avoid them altogether.

Not Taking Required Minimum Distributions

When you contribute to an IRA, the money goes in pre-tax, and you pay tax when you take withdrawals. If there are no withdrawals, there is no tax and that makes Uncle Sam sad. To prevent that, you must take Required Minimum Distributions (RMD) starting at age 73, so Uncle Sam can get his cut. The starting age used to be lower, but it increased by the Secure Act 2 in 2023.

Your first distribution is due by the first day in April, after you turn age 73. All future distributions are due by December 31st of subsequent years. If you miss any of these required distributions, that's going to result in a 25% excise tax. It used to be 50%, but the Secure Act 2 reduced it to 25%. It certainly is an improvement, but it is still a big penalty. Keep in mind that these RMDs are required from all qualified plans such as IRAs, 401(k)s, 403(b)s, TSPs, etc.

Missing a Required Minimum Distribution
is the number one mistake that
qualified plan owners make!

Let's just walk through the math as an example. Let's say, based on the amount of money in your plan and your age, the distribution you are supposed to take in any given year is $10,000. Now, that's your Required Minimum Distribution.

Well, if December 31st came and went, and for whatever reason you failed to take that distribution, here's what will happen: you're still going to need to pay income tax on that distribution. For this example, I'm just estimating the tax to be 30% or $3,000. That obviously will depend on your tax bracket, and you may be in a state where there's also state income tax.

The IRS then goes right back up to that $10,000 missed distribution, and 25% of that becomes an excise tax.

So, if you add together the income tax and the penalty, it's a total of $5,500 of tax and penalty. What does that mean?

$10,000 RMD
$3,000 Tax*
2,500 Penalty
$5,500 to Uncle Sam
$4,500 to You
*30% tax bracket

Out of that $10,000 distribution that was earmarked for your retirement, the IRS wound up with $5,500 of it, and there's only $4500 leftover for you, because you failed to take that distribution timely. It is an expensive mistake that can be easily avoided.

Beneficiary Forms
Not making needed changes in beneficiary forms is another common error. One major problem is assuming that legal documents, such as wills and divorce decrees, created after a beneficiary form is signed, will have the effect of changing the beneficiary. **This is NOT so!** To explain, I am going use a Supreme Court ruling on plan beneficiary forms, and this is the

case of *Kennedy v. Plan Administrator for DuPont Savings and Investment Plan* as an example.

The United States Supreme Court unanimously ruled on January 26, 2009, that William Kennedy's ex-spouse receive his $402,000 retirement plan, because she was the named beneficiary on the beneficiary form. Sounds simple, but it's more complicated than it appears.

They got divorced in 1994, and under the decree of divorce, his ex-spouse waived any rights to any benefits from that retirement plan. It might have been a situation where she got the house and the car, he got the retirement plan and the boat. Anyhow, Mr. Kennedy passed away in 2001.

Now, they had both agreed that the retirement proceeds were to be paid to their only daughter, but Mr. Kennedy and his attorney failed to change the beneficiary document. How could that happen? Well, it's really simple. Both Mr. Kennedy and his attorney believed that because the decree of divorce was a legal document and had a more current date it would override the beneficiary document.

Well, when Mr. Kennedy passed away, the custodian of this $402,000 retirement plan contacted the now ex Mrs. Kennedy and stated: *"We have no choice, we can only pay this to you. How would you like the proceeds paid?"*

She thought about it for a while. *"She's our daughter, and her husband, their kids, the grandkids, they're struggling a little bit, but you know, that $402,000 sure would make my retirement more comfortable."* So, she took possession of the money. The daughter sued her, and it went all the way to the United States Supreme Court, which stated that Mrs. Kennedy, the ex-wife, should receive the $402,000 retirement plan.

This story emphasizes the point: these beneficiary forms are important. They trump everything. It doesn't matter what a will says, what a trust says, or a decree of divorce, or any other signed documents. You really need to make sure your beneficiary forms are set up to do what you want them to do.

Rollovers

When you take money from your qualified plan and deposit it into your bank, it's called a withdrawal, and it's considered taxable income. When you move money from one qualified plan to another qualified plan, it's called a rollover, and it's a **non-taxable event**. If your rollover is done incorrectly, it can make the transfer fully taxable—a big and costly mistake.

A lot of people move money out of their 401(k) when they retire and they change custodians on their IRA, for numerous reasons. Maybe it's to reduce risk or get a higher interest rate. Same thing with TSPs, 403(b)s and 457s. But there are two ways to transfer these qualified plans from one institution to another. One is called a direct rollover; and the other, an indirect rollover.

So, let's take a look at an indirect rollover. Let's say you've got money at risk in the stock market, and you decide to put it in a safer place. So you have your qualified 401(k) plan send you a check. Okay, so now you've got the check. You deposit it. Then you write your check to the new financial institution. No problem, but it has to be done within a 60-day deadline.

Well, so far, so good. But here's where the problem can come into play. You are only allowed to do one indirect rollover every 365 days. If you do an additional rollover during that same 365-day period, that rollover will no longer be qualified, and it's going to be 100% taxable. And most institutions are going to mandatorily withhold 20% for taxes.

Let's take a look at an example. Let's say John has two IRAs, one for $50,000 and the other for $250,000. John does an indirect rollover with a $50,000 IRA in January, and that's perfectly okay. But then three months later, within that 365-day period, John does a second indirect rollover with his $250,000 IRA. And that's not okay. Guess what happened? That second indirect rollover is no longer an IRA, and John now will need to pay income tax on the entire $250,000.

If you're going to move money from one institution to another do a direct rollover. This is what we recommend for all of our clients. That's where the check is sent directly from the current custodian to the new custodian of your choosing.

Same scenario. Maybe you've got money at risk, and you're concerned about what's going to happen to the market, so you want to do a rollover. With a direct rollover, the money is transferred directly from your current financial institution to the new institution of your choosing. It goes directly from one to the other. You don't receive a check. The check is sent directly to the new institution. Or you receive a check, don't deposit it, and send the check to the new institution. That's a direct rollover. And here's the advantage:

You can do this as often as you want, without any tax consequences, and there's no 20% mandatory withholdings. This is why we recommend if you're going to do a rollover, do a direct rollover.

Not Understanding the Secure Act
There are several changes to retirement plan rules under the Secure Act. Some of them good, some of them not. One of the positives is that it eliminates the 70-1/2 age limit for making traditional IRA contributions. Before this, once you turned 70-1/2, you could no longer contribute to your traditional IRA.

That's changed. Now you can contribute as long as you have earned income. What I mean by earned income is income from a job or profits from a business. Other income such as Social Security, interest payments, IRA withdrawals, pension income, etc., do not count.

So, what's the mistake? It's not knowing about a tax advantage with this new rule. You may be able to neutralize the taxes that you have to pay on your required distributions when you start taking money out of these accounts if you have earned income. Here's how that works:

Let's say, based on your age and the amount of money in your IRA, that the distribution that you have to take in any given year comes out to $14,000. Now that's all going to be taxable.

But, because you can continue to make contributions, if you choose to, and you have earned income, you can deposit as much as $14,000 into IRAs. That would be $7000 for your IRA, plus you can deposit an additional $7000 for a non-working spouse, for a total of $14,000.

So, you've got a $14,000 taxable distribution, but you're literally getting a deduction for the $14,000 that you're contributing, so now you have a net zero tax on your required minimum distribution.

Example:
    $14,000 Taxable IRA/401(k) Distribution (RMD)
    - $14,000 Tax Deductible Contribution ($7k + $7k spouse)
    ―――――――――――――――――――――――――――――――――――
    = Zero Net Tax

Now, if your required distribution was over $14,000, the contribution maximum is still going to be $14,000 that you can eliminate the taxes on.

This means, that if you don't need the money from the
Required Minimum Distribution, you can contribute back
up to $14,000 and eliminate the tax. That is, of course, if
you are working and earning enough income to support the
contribution.

There's a couple of rules that have to be followed. To be able to
deposit $7000 for you and $7000 for your spouse:

• You've got to be age 50 and older

• You must have earned income

• You cannot contribute more than your earned income.
  (Social Security, pensions, interest dividends, and rental
  property income are not considered earned income; this
  is just income you're actually earning through a job or
  profits from a business.)

Social Security rarely covers all of your income needs in
retirement; however, it is a vital part of the money you are
entitled to in retirement. That is why it is important to learn the
basics so you make the most out of this benefit. You paid for it,
after all.

Section III

Life Insurance;
The Best Kept Retirement Secret

12 Life Insurance as a Financial Tool

Thanks in advance for actually reading this chapter. I say that because "insurance" is a dirty word to many people. As soon as the word is spoken, all too often they think, "I don't want life insurance, I don't need life insurance, I don't want to think about life insurance." The reason for this is simple: life insurance is often considered "death insurance," because of the death benefit. Most people do not like to think of their own mortality.

Life insurance, however, is far more than just its death benefit. There are many living benefits to life insurance. In fact, is the most misunderstood and under appreciated instrument in financial planning. Life insurance is powerful financial tool with a plethora of benefits that are not familiar to many investors. It may just be the most important feature on the retirement roadmap.

Let's start by defining the various types of insurances. The three prime categories are term insurance, variable life insurance (which means that your money is in the stock market, and thus it is not considered a good vehicle for retirement savings) and permanent cash value life insurance. Permanent cash value life insurance has two types that we will consider for retirement: whole life insurance and indexed universal life insurance (IUL for short).

The most basic form of life insurance is term. It is the classic "death insurance." Designed for affordability, term insurance offers a death benefit for a specific period of time, or term, such as 10 years, 20 years, etc. These types of policies are usually taken out to provide a death benefit to the remaining family for various purposes such as paying off a mortgage or for college bills in the event of an untimely death.

At the end of the term, the policy expires, and if the insurance is to be continued, the policy needs to be renewed, if possible, or replaced. Because the insured is now many years older at the start of the new policy, the new premium will be higher, usually much higher. It could even be unaffordable. For this reason, it is best to purchase the longest possible term, so a renewal is not needed.

The overwhelming majority of term policies lapse without paying a death benefit. It may feel like money wasted, but it would be a proverbial lifesaver if needed.

The type of life insurance that is a good financial tool for retirement is permanent cash value life insurance. There are two types:

• Whole life insurance has a fixed rate of interest that is applied to the policy, year after year. You can set your clock by the amount of money you will make in this policy. You may also receive a dividend. You cannot change the amount of the policy once it's set.

• Indexed universal life, which is a type of universal life insurance, is the other kind of permanent cash value life insurance. It is more flexible that whole life, in that you can change the amount of the policy depending on how your needs change.

As the name implies, the insurance contract is "permanent." This means that instead of purchasing a policy for a limited period of time, the policy is active for the insured's entire life.

In the long run, permanent cash value policies are more cost effective than term policies over the same lifespan. Initial premiums are higher, and depending on the type of insurance you are purchasing—whole life or IUL—the premiums could stay the same or they could change.

There are many features and details of permanent cash value life insurance that I am not going to cover in this book, because going that deep in the weeds won't actually help you understand the primary point that I want to cover: the use of permanent cash value life insurance as a financial tool for retirement savings and income is one of the most valuable and useful you can ever use.

Indexed Universal Life Insurance

So, let's get to the meat of the matter. Indexed Universal Life Insurance is intended primarily for financial growth and offers numerous benefits. It is very flexible. Death benefits , loans, and premiums can all be customized and modified on an ongoing basis as needed.

When properly designed, IULs are a powerful financial tool that offer competitive returns without market risk and lifetime, tax-free income. Yes—you read that right: competitive returns without market risk and lifetime, tax-free income.

An IUL policy (like any other insurance policy) can be designed for a number of purposes, and it takes an expert to do it right. The run-of-the-mill, generalist broker may not be your best choice to help you maximize the benefits of this type of life insurance, and you certainly can't buy these policies online like you can discount auto insurance. It's best to work with a financial professional that specializes in retire planning.
One of IUL's most prominent benefits is financial growth without stock market losses. Simply stated, IULs pay you

interest based on the performance of a stock market index using bonds and options, just as previously described in the indexing section of the chapter, Fill-the-Gap with Guaranteed Income.

You participate in the gains of the stock market without the risk. You will never lose a penny to stock market loss. Every year, you are credited interest and your account balance locks. It will never go down due to crashes. Your principal and interest are protected from market downfalls.

Think for a minute of how beneficial that can be. You are receiving competitive earnings without market loss!

Here are a few financial benefits that IULs offer that most people are not aware of:

Tax Benefits
I talked earlier about the benefits of Roth Conversions. IULs offer the same tax benefits, post-tax contributions as the premiums, and tax-free income. All of these happen without Roth restrictions. There are no income limits and no contribution limits. There are no early withdrawal penalties, and you can get benefits if you are seriously ill. Think of IULs as a giant Roth without any of the Roth limitations.

Lifetime, Tax-Free Income
This is why I think Indexed Universal Life insurance offers the most compelling retirement option. You can combine stock-market crash protection and other benefits with the fact that you can access the account through loans, income tax-free. These loans offer you the ability to create a lifetime, tax-free income stream in retirement.

This is pretty straight forward. All Indexed Universal Life

policies offer this benefit, and with it, it is easy to see that
life insurance can offer benefits that Wall Street simply can't
match. Also, unlike your brokerage account, 401(k), IRA, and
various other accounts, life insurance benefits are tax-free to
your heirs.

Generational Transfer

IULs are a great tool to transfer wealth to the next generation
because you get an instant, leveraged payout when you pass,
all income tax-free. I can't quote exact numbers because actual
policies will perform differently based on current rates, the age
of the insured, and the health of the insured.

Having said that, let's take a look at this realistic possibility:
An insured person in his late 50s places $500,000 in an IUL
designed for maximum growth:

- Depending on numerous factors, the tax-free death benefit
  may be 300% to 400% of the premium.

- Keep in mind, the death benefit can be guaranteed, no ifs,
  ands, or buts.

- If the policy holder passes in five years, the heirs get 3x to
  4x the premium. So, instead of $500k they may get $1.5 or
  even $2 million.

- Even if the policy holder doesn't pass for 20 years, the
  benefit can still be $1.5 or even $2 million.

*Where else can you triple or quadruple your money
in 20 years, guaranteed?*

Long-Term Care

When properly designed, death benefits of an IUL may also
be used to pay for Long-Term Care. The policy benefits may
pay multiples of the premium cost for care, allowing you to
instantly leverage your money which can greatly reduce your

out-of-pocket expenses. This is a great benefit, as 70% of Americans will need nursing care.

Living Benefits

With the proper design, IULs can pay you a portion of your death benefit while you are alive if you have a serious illness. The money can be used for any purpose including medical bills and income replacement.

The majority of bankruptcies in the U.S. are due to medical expenses. When seriously ill, the insured may not be able to work and paying the bills may become a problem. In addition to daily living expenses, medical bills can pile up because your health insurance will not cover all of your medical costs.

Additionally, it is quite common that a spouse needs to take time off to care for the sick spouse, further reducing income. Having access to your insurance benefit while you are alive may prevent severe financial hardships during illnesses.

There you have it. Life insurance is a very powerful tool that can provide financial growth and stability when you need it. But—and you probably guessed that there would be a "but"— you can't get these tools just anywhere. You need to work with a financial professional that understands these plans explicitly and knows how to design them correctly. That's why I strongly advise you to seek a retirement specialist.

The next chapters, *Maximizing Wealth Transfer to the Next Generation* and *Protecting Retirement Income with Life Insurance*, deal with more insurance "fun."

13 Protecting Retirement Income with Life Insurance

Whether in a brokerage account, IRA, 401(k), or any other plan, most Americans have money invested in the stock market that they plan to use for retirement income.

There are numerous theories as to how retirement income should be taken, as well as when and how much. There are too many to discuss, but I going to talk about one, because it's one of the most popular. It's called the 4% rule.

I am quoting *Forbes* from their online article, titled: "What Is The 4% Rule for Retirement Withdrawals?"

> The 4% rule is easy to follow. In the first year of retirement, you can withdraw up to 4% of your portfolio's value. If you have $1 million saved for retirement, for example, you could spend $40,000 in the first year of retirement following the 4% rule.

> Beginning in year two of retirement, you adjust this amount by the rate of inflation. If inflation were 2%, for example, you could withdraw $40,800 ($40,000 x 1.02). In the rare case where prices went down by say 2%, you would withdraw less than the previous year—$39,200 in our example ($40,000 x 0.98). In year three, you'd take the prior year's allowed withdrawal, and then adjust that amount for inflation.

> One common misconception is that the 4% rule dictates

that retirees withdraw 4% of their portfolio's value each year during retirement. The 4% applies only in year one of retirement. After that inflation dictates the amount withdrawn. The goal is to maintain the purchasing power of the 4% withdrawn in the first year of retirement.

Sounds like a well-thought-out plan? Well, the stock market may have something different to say about that.

Let's take a look at this hypothetical example:

Policy Year	Client Age	Index Year	S&P Rate 2001-2018	Interest Credited	Acccount Value BOY	Withdrawals	Account Value EOY
1	60	2001	-14.54	-290,800	2,000,000	0	1,709,200
2	61	2002	-24.87	-425,078	1,709,200	0	1,284,122
3	62	2003	24.88	319.49	1,284,122	0	1,603,612
4	63	2004	7.49	120.111	1,603,612	0	1,723,722
5	64	2005	1.5	25,856	1,723,722	0	1,749,578
6	65	2006	12.12	212,049	1,749,578	0	1,961,627
7	66	2007	2.03	37,501	1,961,627	114,286	1,884.84
8	67	2008	-39.99	-708,045	1,884,842	114.286	1,062,511
9	68	2009	21.95	208,135	1,062,511	114.286	1,156,361
10	69	2010	11.28	117.546	1,156,361	114,286	1,159,621
11	70	2011	-1.5	-15,680	1,159,621	114.286	1,029,655
12	71	2012	11.91	109.02	1,029,655	114,286	1,024,390
13	72	2013	28.1	255,739	1,024,390	114,286	1,165,843
14	73	2014	9.89	103,999	1,165,843	114,286	1,155,557
15	74	2015	-2.23	-23,220	1,155,557	114,286	1,018,051
16	75	2016	8.04	72,663	1,018,051	114,286	976,428
17	76	2017	17.92	154,496	976.428	114,286	1,016,638
18	77	2018	-7.74	-69,842	1,016,638	114.286	832,510
19	78	2001	-14.54	-104,430	832,510	114,286	613,795
20	79	2002	-24.87	-124,228	613,795	114,286	375,281
21	80	2003	24.88	64,936	375,281	114,286	325,931
22	81	2004	7.49	15,852	325,931	114,286	227,497
23	82	2005	1.5	1,698	227,497	114,286	114,910
24	83	2006	12.12	76	114,910	114,286	700
25	84	2007	2.03	0	700	700	0
26	85	2008	-39.99	0	0	0	0
27	86	2009	21.95	0	0	0	0
28	87	2010	11.28	0	0	0	0
29	88	2011	-1.5	0	0	0	0
30	89	2012	11.91	0	0	0	0
31	90	2013	28.1	0	0	0	0
32	91	2014	9.89	0	0	0	0
33	92	2015	-2.23	0	0	0	0
34	93	2016	8.04	0	0	0	0
35	94	2017	17.92	0	0	0	0
36	95	2018	-7.74	0	0	0	0

TOTAL WITHDRAWALS $1,715,333

In this illustration, the client is 60 years old, with $2 million in an IRA brokerage, which is invested in the market, starting in 2001. The actual dollar amount doesn't matter as this concept is identical, no matter what type of account it is or whether the account holds $100,000 or $10 million.

We are using actual S&P returns for years 2001-2018 and repeating them for a total of 36 years. You can see that in the fourth column from the left.

We are showing withdrawals of 4% after tax, per year as income, starting in seven years, at age 66.

Keep in mind, the withdrawals remain at 4% and are not adjusted for inflation as suggested by Forbes in their article. The results would be even worse if we did!

The goal is to create an $80,000 annual cashflow, but since this example uses a qualified account, we need to take out $114,000 to account for taxes. Those withdrawals are shown on the second column from the right.

You can see the stock market had many negative years (fourth column from the left.) We start taking out lifetime withdrawals in Year 7. Now, it's not a good idea to take withdrawals in down years because it cannibalizes the principle, compounding and exacerbating the losses, but since this is the investor's only account, there is no option. The bad news is that the investor is out of money by age 84, indicated by a zero in the far-right column, which is the account value.

Just a 4% net withdrawal, combined with the volatile market, the investor is broke in 25 years. This plan failed the stress test. So much for the 4% rule.

This chapter is titled: "*Protecting Retirement Income with Life Insurance.*" How can life insurance solve this problem, you ask? Read on.

Instead of keeping all $2 million in the market, let's take $600,000 and put it into an IUL (Indexed Universal Life Insurance, which is classified as permanent cash value). The

IUL is designed for maximum growth and income, and it creates what is known as a Buffer Strategy that can offer a hedge against stock market crashes.

The result is that we can increase the amount of money that you will have in retirement and preserve your income.

This next chart is the same brokerage account on the right, but reduced by $600,000.

Brokerage Illustration

Income %:	4.00%		
Portfolio Yr 1:	2,000,000	Tax Bracket:	30%
Level Income:	80,000	Start Year:	7
Cost of Living:	0.0%		

S&P Rate 2001 - 2018 (%)	Withdrawal	Interest Credited	Account Value EOY	Combined Total Withdrawal
(14.54)	200,000	(261,720)	1,538,280	200,000
(24.87)	200,000	(332,830)	1,005,450	260,000
24.88	200,000	200,396	1,005,846	260,000
7.49	0	75,338	1,081,184	60,000
1.50	0	16,218	1,097,401	-
12.12	0	133,005	1,230,406	-
2.03	114,286	22,657	1,138,778	114,286
(39.99)	0	(455,397)	683,381	80,000
21.95	114,286	124,916	694,011	114,286
11.28	114,286	65,393	645,118	114,286
(1.50)	0	(9,677)	635,442	80,000
11.91	114,286	62,070	583,226	114,286
28.10	114,286	131,772	600,712	114,286
9.89	114,286	48,108	534,534	114,286
(2.23)	0	(11,920)	522,614	80,000
8.04	114,286	32,830	441,158	114,286
17.92	114,286	58,575	385,447	114,286
(7.74)	0	(29,834)	355,614	80,000
(14.54)	0	(51,706)	303,908	80,000
(24.87)	0	(75,582)	228,326	80,000
24.88	114,286	28,373	142,413	114,286
7.49	114,286	2,107	30,234	114,286
1.50	30,234	0	0	89,070
12.12	0	0	0	80,000
2.03	0	0	0	80,000
(39.99)	0	0	0	80,000
21.95	0	0	0	80,000
11.28	0	0	0	80,000
(1.50)	0	0	0	80,000
11.91	0	0	0	80,000
28.10	0	0	0	80,000
9.89	0	0	0	80,000
(2.23)	0	0	0	80,000
8.04	0	0	0	80,000
17.92	0	0	0	80,000
(7.74)	0	0	0	80,000
(14.54)	0	0	0	80,000
(24.87)	0	0	0	80,000
24.88	0	0	0	80,000
7.49	0	0	0	80,000
1.50	0	0	0	80,000

This is the illustration for the new IUL:

IUL Illustration

Hypothetical Illustration
Male Age 60 Standard Non-Tobacco
Historical S&P Performance Years 2001 - 2018, Historical Caps & Loan Rates

Hypothetical Indexed Universal Life
Initial Death Benefit: $2,851,704

Policy Year	Age	Index Year	Index Return (%)	Annual Premium	Annual Loan	Accumulation Value EOY	Cash Value EOY	Death Benefit EOY
1	60	2001	0.00	200,000	-	167,427	167,427	3,019,131
2	61	2002	0.00	200,000	60,000	332,490	268,524	3,120,228
3	62	2003	14.00	200,000	60,000	564,988	433,472	3,221,210
4	63	2004	9.00	-	60,000	585,142	382,844	474,726
5	64	2005	4.70	-	-	593,810	380,527	464,243
6	65	2006	13.50	-	-	653,522	429,021	514,825
7	66	2007	2.43	-	-	650,869	414,109	492,790
8	67	2008	0.00	-	80,000	632,717	298,822	352,610
9	68	2009	14.00	-	-	700,569	350,980	410,646
10	69	2010	13.39	-	-	773,720	405,498	470,378
11	70	2011	0.00	-	80,000	776,311	306,216	352,149
12	71	2012	14.00	-	-	887,583	399,766	451,735
13	72	2013	13.00	-	-	1,005,778	500,057	555,063
14	73	2014	13.00	-	-	1,139,608	610,776	665,746
15	74	2015	0.00	-	80,000	1,143,191	511,710	547,530
16	75	2016	10.78	-	-	1,270,348	613,356	644,024
17	76	2017	12.50	-	-	1,433,128	748,213	785,624
18	77	2018	0.00	-	80,000	1,437,362	639,939	671,936
19	78	2001	0.00	-	80,000	1,441,678	501,431	526,503
20	79	2002	0.00	-	80,000	1,446,051	358,365	376,284
21	80	2003	14.00	-	-	1,652,581	498,655	523,588
22	81	2004	9.00	-	-	1,805,451	586,560	615,888
23	82	2005	4.70	-	58,836	1,894,469	547,361	574,729
24	83	2006	13.50	-	80,000	2,153,897	651,723	684,309
25	84	2007	2.43	-	80,000	2,210,076	541,516	568,592
26	85	2008	0.00	-	80,000	2,213,652	370,494	389,019
27	86	2009	14.00	-	80,000	2,525,895	512,349	537,967
28	87	2010	13.39	-	80,000	2,865,887	660,755	693,793
29	88	2011	0.00	-	80,000	2,867,876	471,230	494,791
30	89	2012	14.00	-	80,000	3,269,117	699,100	734,055
31	90	2013	13.00	-	80,000	3,692,682	945,411	992,681
32	91	2014	13.00	-	80,000	4,171,633	1,215,155	1,263,761
33	92	2015	0.00	-	80,000	4,172,711	1,023,276	1,053,975
34	93	2016	10.78	-	80,000	4,624,416	1,264,512	1,289,802
35	94	2017	12.50	-	80,000	5,206,980	1,620,879	1,637,088
36	95	2018	0.00	-	80,000	5,214,487	1,392,578	1,392,578
37	96	2001	0.00	-	80,000	5,220,828	1,039,542	1,039,542
38	97	2002	0.00	-	80,000	5,225,841	682,884	682,884
39	98	2003	14.00	-	80,000	5,960,962	1,056,467	1,056,467
40	99	2004	9.00	-	80,000	6,499,268	1,234,145	1,234,145
41	100	2005	4.70	-	80,000	6,804,671	1,169,308	1,169,308

This illustration is not NAIC compliant and assumes current charges and index rates of return as indicated. Actual results may be more or less favorable than those shown.

You can see the three $200,000 premium payments that were transferred to the IUL from the IRA here in the fifth column from the left, "Annual Premium," on the IUL Illustration.

With a 30% tax rate, we will need to take $60,000 out of the IUL in Years 2, 3, and 4 to pay the taxes. You can see those three withdrawals in the sixth column from the left, Annual Loan. This tax money will come from the IUL as a policy loan and thus will not need to be paid out of pocket.

This example is for an IRA, but the Buffer Strategy will work with any type of account.

Going back to the Brokerage Account Illustration, we are still withdrawing the $114,000 a year, but this time, we are only taking the withdrawals in years that the stock market is positive. There are no withdrawals from the IRA brokerage account in the years that the stock market crashes.

Instead, we are taking money from the IUL in years that the stock market crashes. And you can see those in the sixth column from the left, Annual Loan, in the IUL Illustration.

You can see that where there are zero withdrawals on the right from the brokerage account, we have withdrawals on the left from the IUL.

Now, you can see that with the combination of withdrawals and stock market crashes, the brokerage account is dry at age 82. In other words, the client's brokerage account is out of money by age 82, but look at the IUL. In addition to all the annual $80,000 tax-free withdrawals to age 100, there is still $540,00 in the cash value at age 85, $945,000 at age 90, $1.3 million at age 95, and nearly the same at age 100 as shown in Column 8.

This is how we stop financial plans from failing the stress test. The IUL Buffer Strategy can prevent you from running out of money in retirement. Life insurance for the win.

IUL's Secret Sauce
In addition to protecting your account from market risk, there's a secret sauce to IULs that are not, and cannot, be matched by any other financial tool.

You may have noticed that the withdrawals from the IUL in the sixth column, are titled Annual Loans. When you take money out of the IUL it is done as a loan from the insurance company, not your account. The money in your account stays put.

Here's why that is so valuable:

1) Since it is a loan against your death benefit, and death benefits are income tax-free, your loans are income tax-free.

2) Loans do not have to be paid back during your lifetime. They can be, but if you don't pay back the loan, then the balance of the loan comes out of your death benefit when you pass. The death benefits shown in the illustration above, in Column 9, already subtracted the loans that were to be paid back to the company.

3) You still earn interest on the money that you borrow. Read that again; you still earn interest on the money that you borrow.

When taking a loan, you are borrowing from the insurance company, not your account. Because of that, you are still earning interest on your full account balance as if you never took any loans. Column 8 is your cash in the account, but

Column 7 is the amount that you are earning interest on—the amount as if you never took loans.

If you have $100,000 in your account and you took a $25,000 loan, your account remains at $100,000 and you earn interest on the full $100,000.

You will pay the insurance company interest on your $25,000 loan and they will credit you interest on your full $100,000 account balance.

The loan rate continuously varies, but let's use 5% as an example. If you pay 5% on your loan, and you are credited 11% for the year, you just earned 6% on money you borrowed. Imagine going to the bank and asking them for a loan where they pay you interest!

Every year, for the rest of your life, you will earn interest on the arbitrage, a fancy term that means the difference between what your loan costs and the amount that the insurance company credits you, which is determined by market performance.

In the years that your interest credit is lower than your interest rate, the loan will cost you the difference between the two. In the years that your credit is higher than your interest rate, you will be credited interest on money that you borrowed.

Given the market's history, there are more years are up than down, this is yet another win for life insurance.

14 Maximizing Wealth Transfer to the Next Generation

It is an important question to ask yourself: do you want your funds to be used for your retirement or do you want them, or part of them, to go to your children as an inheritance?

I ask because if you want to create legacy, permanent cash value life insurance is a great way to maximize wealth transfer to the next generation.

Case Study: Mark and Nancy

Mark and Nancy are 60. They planned well, and they have a comfortable retirement income. They have a sum of money they want leave to their daughter Rebecca as an inheritance to pay for college for their grandchildren.

We showed them how an IUL policy works as a powerful financial tool to transfer wealth to the next generation. It contains a few great benefits that they weren't aware of: the money given to Rebecca will be dramatically higher than what they contribute, the amount is guaranteed, it has zero stock market risk, and this great benefit is all income-tax free.

Life insurance is life insurance because it has a death benefit. That death benefit is the great benefit, and it is one of the most effective means of wealth transfer available.

Life insurance, when properly designed, is a very powerful financial tool that can transfer wealth to the next generation with a guaranteed inheritance that's tax free. Unlike money that you may be saving for your kids and grandchildren in the stock market, there is no stock market risk. The result is that the life insurance inheritance could be substantially higher than your stock market account.

Let's take a closer look at some numbers. The amount that Mark and Nancy have set aside in a brokerage account for their daughter is $500,000. At 60 years of age, their average life expectancy is 27 years. Based on the average performance of the stock market, their investment should grow an average of 5.5% per year over that time. Granted, some years will be higher, some will be lower, and some will include losses. And sure, recently we've had some great years. But over the lifetime of the market, 5.5% is the average overall performance, even when market crashes are factored in.

Over time, their account will grow nicely, but, that money will not be free and clear when inherited. Rebecca will need to pay income tax. Uncle Sam is going to take 35 to 37% of her inheritance, plus her tax bracket will increase for all her family's income that year, which doesn't even show up in these calculations.

Comparing Numbers
Now let's see how that compares to life insurance with the same $500,000 as a premium. We are going to use a second-to-die policy for Mark and Nancy which comes out to about $1.7 million of coverage. I say "about" because the actual coverage will depend on several factors, including health. I used non-smoking, standard health rates for this example. Keep in mind, that the earlier in life you start the policy, the higher the benefits will be.

Now I want to compare their brokerage account balance to the life insurance amount ten years later, when they reach age 70.

At that point the brokerage account will be at $572,000 after taxes, compared to about $1.7 million for the insurance policy. At age 80, the brokerage account will be $926,000 versus about $1.7 million. And if we look at 85 and 87, which are the average life expectancies for men and women, the brokerage account will be $1.2 million and $1.3 million versus $1.7 million for the life insurance. Life insurance for the win.

Other Benefits

One major concern that those brokerage numbers didn't reveal is market crashes. As previously stated, the 120-year history of the stock market shows us that it crashes an average of 47% every 11 years. You may see several market crashes in your future that could dramatically lower the value of your brokerage account, especially if it happens right before you pass. However, life insurance is not affected in any way by stock-market declines. Depending on the date you pass, the difference could be astounding.

Another benefit in the payout phase is an immediate multiple of the initial cost. If the insured passes quickly after purchase, the heirs get a very large benefit compared to the cost. Even if the benefit isn't paid out for 20 years, the benefit is still highly multiplied over the cost.

Overall, life insurance is a much better financial tool than most people realize. It works amazingly well for retirement, and you're able to ensure your heirs have benefits when you pass.

Those who say that life insurance isn't a good financial tool usually are the very same people who want to make money for themselves by putting you in the stock market, so they can earn fees even when you lose money. If your money is in an insurance policy, they make nothing. Remember that as you read upcoming chapters.

Section IV

Read No Evil

CHAPTER

15 The Internet Is Not Your Friend

Many of you reading this book will fall into an age bracket similar to mine. For most of your life, you relied on sources of information such as encyclopedias, Yellow Pages, and TV Guides. Remember those relics?

Today, you might find those remnants in a museum. But you are extremely unlikely to find those in print anywhere in your house anymore. The Internet has taken over as the go-to source for just about everything from information to entertainment. For many people, the Internet, accessed through our phones and tablets, have replaced the need for TV altogether. Find yourself bored? You now have YouTube, Netflix, Amazon Prime Video, Apple TV, and dozens of other options that can consume every idle moment you have in your day, if you let them.

Some of us can remember when the Internet was in its infancy. There were very few websites, graphics were terrible, and information was hard to locate. We've come a long way, considering most people today are dubious of any company that doesn't have a website and multiple social media channels. And we all know someone who believes society will cease to exist without the Internet.

But with the explosive growth of the Internet, the world has been given instant access to two distinct categories of information: 1) helpful information, and 2) misinformation.

And unfortunately, there's no label at the top of the page! The real danger is when the source contains both. While it's nearly incomprehensible how much information is accessible online, the amount of misinformation is even more staggering. Anyone can "publish" anything online with no regard for morals, facts, or biases. There is no longer an editor or publisher to ensure accuracy or truth.

Worse yet, there's no longer a cooling-off period, during which you can "stop the presses" to retract misstatements or harmful dialogue. Rather, we live in a "Type and Send" society. The span between thinking, typing, and publishing can be mere seconds. As Mitch Ratcliffe has observed, "A computer lets you make more mistakes faster than any invention in human history, with the possible exceptions of handguns and tequila."[13]

Flush with Information—Flooded with Misinformation
Where does this leave us? In my opinion, we are flush with information and flooded with misinformation. John Wanamaker, founder of America's first department store, once said, "Half my advertising spend is wasted; the trouble is, I don't know which half."[14] (Yes, I used the Internet to look this up to get the source and exact wording. And then I double- and triple-checked it because we all know how reliable the Internet can be.)

I have updated the adage to describe the Internet. My version is, "I know 90% of what is on the Internet is wrong, I just don't know which 10% is right." While it may be exaggerated and meant more as humor, it is not far off. As I said, the amount of misinformation available on the web is staggering.

I offer one of my favorite Internet finds as an example:

Petition
to Ban
DHMO

What is Dihydrogen Monoxide?
- DHMO is a colorless, odorless chemical compound
- Used as an industrial coolant
- Accelerates corrosion and rusting of many metals
- Used as distributing agent in pesticides
- Effective as fire retardant
- Most alarming, it is found in most many foods

Why Ban DHMO?
- Ingestion can cause nausea and vomiting
- Deadly if accidentally inhaled
- It is a major component of acid rain
- It has been linked to global climate change
- Many industries dump waste DHMO into the ocean
- It has been found in almost all cancer biopsies

For more information on HMO visit: http://www.dhmo.org

The content is as truthful as it is deceitful. The dichotomy doesn't become apparent until you realize that Dihydrogen Monoxide is water. Sneaky, huh? Well, that's the Internet for you.

The duality of the Internet, fact versus fiction, applies as much to the subjects of retirement and financial planning as it does to so many other subjects. So much of the information found online is biased, wrong, outdated, or not applicable to the majority of situations. In other words, even if it was written with the best of intentions, it can be misleading. And I haven't even touched on the scoundrels who are out to intentionally deceive you. There should be a special place in hell for those people.

To offer some personal perspective, I end my initial client presentation meetings with this: "I want you to understand and be comfortable with the concepts and plan that I have presented But, I have one favor to ask. Don't go out and Google anything... yet. Google (or any search engine for that matter) will give you great results and terrible results. If you are not already knowledgeable about the content, you know won't know which ones are accurate. Please review the educational materials that I provided to you before you Google them. This way you will have a better idea of what questions to ask and a better understanding of what answers you'll find. Sound fair?"

To boil this chapter down to one sentence: "Get the facts from a financial professional before researching on your own."

Sound fair?

Section V

Why the Stock Market
is Not a Good Retirement Strategy

16 What Wall Street Is Not Telling You About the Stock Market

Wall Street is complex and unpredictable. And it's no secret that it can also be full of hidden costs. These costs, coupled with poor financial advice, can rip off investors. That in turn hurts you in retirement.

I'll name the Top Ten concerns not talked about, and explain.

Hiding Fees in Small Print
Small print has been going on as long as paper has been printed. The general reasoning is it saves paper. But it can also hide fees and costs. You'll also see it used in the digital world as you scroll through and check off customer agreements on the Internet. And if you are like a lot of the people I meet, you may not have the time or patience to read and understand what they mean.

Admittedly, some stockbrokers, financial advisors, and even mutual funds charge investors as much as 1% to 2% per year. And if your portfolio gains 10%, it might seem reasonable to pay that much a year in fees. But, look at this way; 1% annual fee on a 10% growth, means you are paying them 10% of your profits! If you earn just 5%, you are paying them 20% of your profits, and when the market crashes and you lose money, they still take their 1% from your account. They may money even when you lose.

And, if general inflation happens to climb past 5%, as it has many times, it will mean a buying power return that is much lower. Even a 10% gain might end up being only 3% in your pocket. This means as much as 66% of your profits will go to fees and inflation. Even with low gains and low inflation, the same math will apply.

In addition to the stated brokerage fees, there will be other hidden fees and charges. Even with a "no fee account"—yes, those do exist—there will be hidden costs. Some investors try to keep track of every expense to control costs, but this is almost impossible, since they don't show up on your statements.

A 2009 study found that the average trading costs for thousands of U.S. mutual funds was 1.44% more than their stated expenses.[15] I did some poking around to find a more recent stat, but to no avail.

Brokerage fees can make up a significant percentage of these hidden costs. The SEC requires that the total amount of brokerage fees be disclosed, but these fees are often not translated into the expense ratio. These hidden costs can also include the bid/ask spread of stocks. (Bid/ask is a two-way price quotation that indicates the best potential price at which a security can be sold and bought at a given point in time.)

This is where a professional financial advisor can be invaluable in outlining the costs associated with your investments. Even if you have the patience to read between the lines, you may still find the information confusing.

Too Much Diversification
Diversification of your investment can help balance market losses, but a large portfolio of mutual funds can add additional, unneeded expenses to your investments. Diversified portfolios are constructed of thousands of different assets in hundreds

of different countries around the world. Even if you believe you will achieve a balance of risk, you will still be open to the world we live in, where there is a greater potential for unethical and corrupt financial entities.

Many investors believe that greater diversification will lead to higher risk-adjusted returns. This theory can give a false assurance to passive investors. In reality, over-diversification can make portfolios more expensive and harder to manage. There really is no reason to invest in hundreds or thousands of stocks, across asset classes and countries.

Diversification also limits your upside. When a small investment asset grows by 50%, your portfolio may only grow by one percent. Whereas, if you place 20% of your money in that same asset class, your return will be much, much higher. Of course, there is no asset class or investment that is completely "risk free," but I find professional guidance and advice to be a better way to manage your personal risk tolerance than over-diversification.

I also want to add that being diversified does not protect you from general market trends. Assets don't necessarily move counter to each other during rough times. It's far more common for asset classes to go down together.

I believe it is better to limit your portfolio to ten or twelve assets that you truly understand. This is exactly what many of the smartest and most successful investors in the world do. Additionally, an overload of multiple small print reports being sent to you every quarter can be confusing at best.

Nominal Returns versus Real Returns
A nominal rate of return is the amount of money generated by an investment before factoring in expenses such as 1) taxes, 2)

investment fees, and 3) inflation. If an investment generated a 10% return, the nominal rate would equal 10%.

But real returns represent a more accurate picture. Although there may be nominal investment gains from interest on savings accounts, and from bonds, dividends, and capital gains, real returns are more often affected by costs. Knowing these costs before you choose an investment instrument will provide a higher rate of real return.

Preparing for these three expenses can improve your returns.

Taxes:
The first one, taxes, can be an unknown and an April surprise. This is where professional advisors and accountants can help. They should be consulted before your portfolio is reinvested or distributed. You will always be taxed on the profits.

Investment Fees:
Investment fees, which I've already covered, need to be questioned and studied. As I mentioned, these fees can be hidden in the small print and costly to your investment profits.

Inflation:
Inflation can be real killer, especially if your wages are not keeping up or you are retired and on a fixed income. As I am writing this in 2023, gas and food prices have risen higher than anyone predicted, far higher than the published inflation rate, and will affect the budget of every American family.

When nominal returns are adjusted for these costs and other unknowns, your real returns might surprise you.

Active versus Passive Investor
When an investment portfolio becomes complex, investors

tend to feel less involved and more complacent. I have seen this many times. People will be very engaged when we first meet, but over time will be less interested in the large amount of information I will need to provide. I've seen their eyes gloss over with each additional document.

Small investors can frequently become passive investors, especially when they have never owned a business or stuck to a budget. I encourage all of you who read this section to take your investments seriously and take an active role when it involves your money.

In today's digital world, that will mean setting up an online account that can be checked on a regular basis. I also recommend keeping abreast of financial news, such as changes in the Fed rate and inflation numbers.

When you take an active role in your portfolio, you will stay on top of your investment future.

Money Markets are Not the Same as Cash

A money market fund is a type of mutual fund that invests in high-quality cash equivalents or short-term debt instruments. In some cases, they are not FDIC insured, and therefore not as safe as cash. However, they are an extremely low-risk investment and can be advantageous if you need a short-term, relatively safe place to park cash.

Most traditional savings accounts offer nominal interest rates, so I sometimes suggest that money market funds or Money Market Accounts are a better alternative, as they typically offer higher returns.

As I write this, I am seeing rates as high as 4.03% and as low as 0.01%. My advice is to check with your bank or credit union and see what they offer. Money markets can be great way to safely grow your portfolio.

Bonds versus Equities

Bonds are supposed to be your safety net. It's what all the financial professionals tout as the most "effective" and "diversified" portfolio: you put 60% of your money in stocks and 40% of your money in bonds.

But what happens when the bond market crashes? Your money may or may not be "safe," like people who have come to me because they notice the bond side of their portfolio isn't moving.

There are different kinds of bonds: corporate bonds, government bonds, municipal bonds, bond funds, and bond index funds. Most people do not understand them and for good reason. They can be confusing.

To talk about all of them would take an entire book. For purposes of this chapter, I'm going to talk about corporate bonds. On the surface, they are like stocks: they both allow businesses to fund their operations. The main differences between these two are the agreements made with investors and the amount they pay out.

Stocks will have a stronger top-end return on investments, whereas bonds will have a capped return, meaning that you only earn as much as the corporate bond advertises. Even if a small company does well and their stock climbs accordingly, their bonds will not reflect that gain. This is because bond growth results from a company reinvesting in itself.

As I said above, bonds are not fail-safe. They may be less risky than equities, but just like stocks, there is no guarantee you will get all your money back.

And it's worth noting that bond prices fall when interest rates go up. As inflation has risen, the Fed has responded with a higher interest rate. As I type this, the rate is now between 4.25% and 4.5% and may go up. These higher interest rates will affect bond returns, which are generally running a little over a 1% return as I write this.[16] A 1% return is not sound retirement planning.

Sales Commissions/Fees

Unless otherwise stated, all products come with a sales commission/fee. Any salesman knows this. When certain products are recommended by a financial advisor, I believe it is imperative that the advisor also go over the commissions/fees they will earn from those sales. This is what a professional would do.

It is also important here to understand the differences between commissions and fees, at least in the way these words are used in the financial services industry. A commission-based advisor makes money by selling investment products, whereas a fee-based advisor will charge a flat rate for managing a client's money. This may either be a dollar amount or a percentage of assets under management (AUM is the funds managed by investment advisors)

In the financial services sector, insurance commissions will generally fall between 2% and 8% of the premium, depending on state regulations.

For mutual funds, advisors generally receive a trailer fee, which is a fixed percentage of a client's investment. They can also receive payments that come from the front or back-end loads. This is a fee that is charged when shares are bought or sold.

Some investments may not be appropriate for your portfolio; but because they provide enormous sales commissions/fees, unscrupulous advisors may recommend them. This is why it is important to work with a true financial professional. And this is yet another reason why you should have an active interest in your money.

Stock Picking and Transaction Costs
I have yet to see a financial professional who can pick stocks perfectly. The obvious formula is to buy low and sell high. But I have always been skeptical of any advisor who claims to be good at it, and you should be too. The adage "don't put all your eggs in one basket" is especially important here. Picking just a few stocks because someone recommended them, or worse yet, because you read about it on the Internet, can be the worst investment you will ever make.

It is also important to discuss the fees a stock transaction might cost. When considering an advisor, look at the full list of commissions/fees they will charge, and be wary of those who appear interested in selling products just for commissions/fees rather than for your best interest. Today, most brokers, especially online brokers, no longer charge a commission for buying or selling stocks.

Making it All About the Money
If you have picked the best professional to manage your finances, you will have picked someone who is not only interested in your money, but also in your health, your risk tolerance, your employment benefits, the expectations of your spouse, your kids' and grandkids' future, and, most importantly, your long-term retirement plans. Your financial advisor may not be your best friend, but they need to have your best interests at heart.

In today's digital world, there are many ways to evaluate an advisor. I recommend using online reviews to decide on a good professional fit. I also believe in personal interviews and healthy skepticism.

Being Overly Optimistic

I frequently meet people who believe the best investments are right around the corner, and they expect to get in on the ground floor. For example, many believed that when the COVID pandemic was over, the market would surge. The opposite happened.

Some are convinced that when interest rates start coming down, there will be a short-term surge in the market and they want to be in on it.

Or when inflation eases

Or when housing is affordable

Or when people get back to work

Or when all their debts are paid

You can expand this list ad nauseum. But the market doesn't always respond, and it's always a steep uphill climb out of the hole a down market dug for your retirement nest egg.

The truth is investors, and sometimes advisors, have a natural interest in hoping for a better market and a better future. Just like New Year's resolutions, you always hope for a better tomorrow. However, the track record is mixed. More often than not, there will be unforeseen events, including personal losses that will challenge your investment future.

In Conclusion

Wall Street is complex and unpredictable. Your best investment strategy is to find an advisor who will take the time to understand what you and your family want and need, and who will be open and honest about what he or she can provide.

17 The Failure of Diversification and Low-Risk Investing

No matter how much you know about how volatile the stock market is, and why it's not a safe bet at all, it is still the number one place for people to put their retirement funds. If you still want to continue using the stock market as the primary way for you to make money on the money you put into it, then read on.

Two popular strategies commonly used to reduce risk and losses are portfolio diversification and low-risk investing. Both are viable options, but their benefits are often misunderstood.

The concept of a diversified portfolio is spreading investments across different asset classes, industries, and/or geographies to mitigate the risk of losses from stock market crashes in any one area. Investments can be spread across various sectors such as technology, health, energy, etc. It may also mean both domestic and international funds. Likewise, it could include different types of investments such as stocks, bonds, metals, real estate, etc.

However, despite the concept's advantages, a diversified portfolio does not guarantee profit, and it does not guarantee protection.

Market crashes can affect all asset classes and types, including those that are traditionally seen as less risky. For example, during the 2008 financial crisis, the stock market was not the only asset class to experience downfalls. Bonds, real estate, and commodities also experienced significant declines. No asset class is immune to market downturns.

Additionally, diversification does not always work as expected. There are times when different asset classes move in tandem, making diversification less effective. The 2008 financial crisis is one of the more recent examples. Many different asset classes declined in value at the same time.

The second concept is low-risk stocks, so let's dive into that a bit. When researching stocks, you will find they are often classified with an associated risk level. High-risk versus low-risk is a descriptor of their volatility. It is also commonly associated with their profit potential. The lower the risk, typically, the lower the return. You may reduce risk, but you are likewise sacrificing earnings.

The term "low risk" is relative. What may be considered a low-risk stock in one market environment may be considered high-risk in another. During a market downturn, even stocks that are considered to be low-risk may decline in value as investors sell off their holdings to minimize losses.

While low-risk stocks may have a lower volatility than high-risk stocks, they are still subject to market forces such as changes in interest rates, economic conditions, and investor sentiment. During market crashes, these factors can drive down the value of low-risk stocks, resulting in losses for investors.

Low-risk stocks may also be impacted by sector-specific risks. For example, a low-risk stock in the utilities sector may be vulnerable to changes in energy prices or regulations, while a low-risk stock in the healthcare sector may be impacted by changes in healthcare policy. As a result, even low-risk stocks can be impacted by events that are specific to their sector, leading to declines in value during a market crash.

If you say to your advisor that you are concerned with risk, most will probably suggest diversification and low-risk stocks.

Just one more thing Wall Street isn't telling you.

18 Sequence of Returns Can Devastate Your Retirement

There is one more thing Wall Street keeps quiet about, and it is the most devastating thing that can happen to your retirement funds. It's called *"Sequence of Returns Risk."* Some call it timing risk.

Whatever the name, it's when you take a distribution from your funds in a down market, and can leave you with not enough money to make it through your retirement years.

The five years before retirement and the five years after retirement are the most critical when it comes to stock market performance.

Here's why: While well-known to financial professionals, most investors have not heard the concept of *Sequence of Returns*. The concept illustrates that the order in which your portfolio gains or loses can dramatically affect its value when you are in the distribution phase.

I am going to use stock market returns from 2000 to 2020 for this example in the following charts. For this discussion, let's call 2000 the start of your retirement, and 2020 the later part in your retirement.

Sequence of Return Risk...Accumulation

	2000	-10.14%	$179,720	16.26%	$232,520
	2001	-13.04%	$156,285	28.88%	$299,672
$200,000 Invested	**2002**	-23.37%	$119,761	-6.24%	$280,972
	2003	26.38%	$151,354	19.42%	$335,537
	2004	8.99%	$164,960	9.54%	$367,547
No Withdrawals	**2005**	3%	$169,909	-0.73%	$364,864
	2006	13.62%	$193,051	11.39%	$406,422
	2007	3.53%	$199,866	29.60%	$526,723
	2008	-38.49%	$122,937	13.41%	$597,357
Regardless of the	**2009**	23.45%	$151,766	0%	$597,357
sequence of returns,	**2010**	12.78%	$171,162	12.78%	$673,699
your balance is the	**2011**	0%	$171,162	23.45%	$831,681
same	**2012**	13.41%	$194,115	-38.49%	$511,567
	2013	29.60%	$251,573	3.53%	$529,626
	2014	11.39%	$280,227	13.62%	$601,761
	2015	-0.73%	$278,181	3%	$619,813
	2016	9.54%	$304,719	8.99%	$675,535
	2017	19.42%	$363,896	26.38%	$853,741
	2018	-6.24%	$341,189	-23.37%	$654,221
	2019	28.88%	$439,724	-13.04%	$568,911
	2020	16.26%	**$511,223**	-10.14%	**$511,223**

The second column from the left lists the actual returns of the S&P from 2000 to 2020, in the order they happened. The next column to its right lists the results of the market performance on the account with a starting balance of $200,000. By 2020, the account would have grown to $511,223.

The two columns on the right side are the results of flip-flopping the order of the stock market returns. You will notice that regardless of the sequence of the profits and losses in the market, the balance is the same, $511,223.

During the accumulation phase, when you are not withdrawing funds, the sequence of returns does not matter.

But—and again, this is a big "but"—you will notice quite a difference in the next graphic.

Sequence of Return Risk...Withdrawals

	2000	-10.14%	$169,720	16.26%	$222,520
	2001	-13.04%	$137,589	28.88%	$276,784
$200,000 Invested	**2002**	-23.37%	$95,434	-6.24%	$249,512
	2003	26.38%	$110,610	19.42%	$287,968
$10,000 Annual	**2004**	8.99%	$110,553	9.54%	$305,440
Withdrawals	**2005**	3%	$103,870	-0.73%	$293,210
During Retirement	**2006**	13.62%	$108,017	11.39%	$316,607
(5% of initial balance)	**2007**	3.53%	$101,830	29.60%	$400,322
	2008	-38.49%	$52,636	13.41%	$444,006
	2009	23.45%	$54,979	0%	$434,006
	2010	12.78%	$52,005	12.78%	$479,472
Early Market Losses	**2011**	0%	$42,005	23.45%	$581,908
Can Devastate	**2012**	13.41%	$37,638	-38.49%	$347,931
Your Account!	**2013**	29.60%	$38,779	3.53%	$350,213
	2014	11.39%	$33,196	13.62%	$387,913
	2015	-0.73%	$22,953	3%	$389,550
	2016	9.54%	$15,143	8.99%	$414,570
	2017	19.42%	$8,084	26.38%	$513,934
	2018	-6.24%	$0	-23.37%	$383,828
	2019	28.88%	$0	-13.04%	$323,777
	2020	16.26%	$0	-10.14%	$280,946

This chart shows the same $200,000 invested, but this time taking $10,000 annual withdrawals.

Take a look at the third column from the left with actual stock market performance in the proper order. By year 2018, the account balance on the left is zero!

In contrast, the two columns on the right show the S&P performance reversed and the results. Instead of heavy losses in the first three years of retirement, the losses occur near the end, and profits are near the beginning. The difference is amazing. Instead of a zero balance in 2018, there is $383,828 in the account. Despite two more years of significant losses, the investor still has $280,946 by the end of 2020.

Of course, we can't flip-flop the returns or control them in any way, but the reason that I am showing this is that if you take losses near the beginning of your retirement, while taking withdrawals, you will have less money than if those losses happen later in retirement.

Here's the problem. In 2023, when this book was written, we are starting at the top of the first two columns. The S&P dropped 18% in 2022, and 2023 may witness further drops. The history of the market shows that it drops 47% every 11 years on average. If you don't get your money out of the market and stop the losses, you will likely have less money down the road.

This shows why it is critical to protect your account from losses in retirement, especially within the five years before and the five years after retirement.

Section VI

Is Your Financial Advisor Right For You?

19 Is Your Advisor an Advisor?

A common definition for the term "advisor" is someone who gives advice. Sounds simple, except when it comes to "financial advisors." I find that many so called "financial advisors" are not. They are better described as fee collectors.

Here are some thoughts to peruse in order to help you figure out which kind of advisor you have:

Did your "advisor" actually create a long-term financial plan for your family that includes paying for college, long-term goals, market loss protection, inflation protection, tax reduction, retirement income, long-term care needs and death of a spouse? Or, did he/she just sell you stocks, bonds and/or mutual funds?

When the market dropped in the beginning of 2022, did your "advisor" call you with suggested changes to your plan to protect your wealth from the downturn?

What about mid-2022 when the market continued to drop? Did your "advisor" call you with suggested changes to your plan to protect your wealth from the downturn?

What about the end of 2022 when the market was still dropping? Did your "advisor" call you with suggested changes to your plan to protect your wealth from the downturn?

In those all those down months, did your advisor ever call with suggested changes to your plan?

Did they put a plan in place to prevent future losses?

When the market is down, does your advisor say "It's a great time to buy?" When the market is up, does your advisor say "It's a great time to buy?" Ever wonder why, that no matter what the market does, your "advisor" always wants you to buy?

Your advisor makes money when you buy, and when you are in the market. Your advisor makes money when you profit, and your advisor makes money when you lose money. Sounds like a better "financial plan" for the advisor than for you.

I know my vehicle mechanic is honest. The reason that I know that is on more than one occasion over the years, he has told me that I don't need a repair that I thought that I did. He only makes money when he does a repair and has actually said, "Don't spend the money." Ever heard those words from your advisor?

On the flip side, there are "advisors" who suggest changes constantly because they receive large commissions/fees for every trade, both on the "buy" and on the "sell" side. They are the ones who see "market indicators" that say the market is about to drop so you should sell to avoid the drop, only to have you buy again when the "indicators" dictate. Funny how often those "indicators" pop up.

If your "financial advisor" is merely a fee collector, it may be time to find a financial professional who puts your needs first.

What to Look for When Choosing a Financial Professional

Before we begin to talk about choosing a financial professional, I want to relay a conversation that I had with a couple.

Case Study: Robert and Deborah

Robert was a mechanic and Deborah was a bookkeeper. They were in their mid-50s. They had just finished paying off the loans they had taken out to put their two kids through college, and retirement was getting closer and very much on their minds. They contacted me to talk about their retirement account because they were concerned when their balance significantly dropped. They were down over $50,000.

I spent quite a bit of time talking to them about market risk and crashes. The look on their faces can only be described as fright. They knew their account was dropping, but they truly didn't understand the short- and long-term risks of the stock market. They were just a few years from retirement and very concerned that more losses would derail their plans to travel and spend time with their future grandkids.

I explained that in their younger, working years, growth and accumulation were important, but now that they were closer to retirement, it was vital to shift their goals to protection and income, so crashes would not destroy their retirement.

Younger investors can weather market crashes, but the closer they get to their retirement date, the more devastating crashes can be. I then showed Robert and Deborah how they could earn stock-market-like profits in an account that was protected, no matter what a happened in the market. They were elated!

I could tell that they didn't want to say it, but they finally admitted they were talking to several other financial professionals at the same time that they were speaking with me. They shared that because none of the other professionals had talked about risks and losses like I had. They said that they were glad to finally find a professional that not only explained the risks, but also shared a solution to protect their retirement from crashes.

The Bottom Line

Turning to the crux of the issue: choosing a financial professional can be a very difficult decision. You are trusting decades of your work and hard-earned savings with this individual and the scary part is there is no clear-cut way of determining what they may or may not do for you in the future. You may not even know what questions to ask, so you end up having to make vital financial decisions based on hunches.

Prospective advisors will happily tell you about their education and background, how long they have been in the business, the amount of assets they have under management, the number of clients they have, etc., etc. They will tell you what they want you to hear, but the question is will they tell you what you need to know? Here's a question to ask yourself that many people overlook: did the prospective advisor tell you the whole story when it comes to the stock market?

Investing is a high gamble and is sometimes very risky. We see that yet again with the current high volatility in the market.

Risk not only includes a gamble on specific stocks and mutual funds, but on the overall market as well. Market crashes can take down any stock or mutual fund, even if it is considered a low-risk investment.

Ever hear I hear the expression *"My 401(k) has turned into a 201(k)?" It's a funny expression that has a lot of truth to it and you hea*r that a lot every time the market crashes. And it's not just your 401(k). IRAs, brokerage accounts and other plans can also crash right alongside a 401(k).

Mitigating risk while increasing profit is the goal of most investors. So, I ask again, did your financial professional discuss risk and market crashes with you? Did they show you the history of the stock market and how it crashes 47% every 11 years on average? Did he or she tell you we are far past that 11-year average and are expecting major crashes? Even if we do not know when these crashes will happen, the fact still remains that a major market crash is on the way.

Did they mention that the average time it takes to break even from a major crash is over six years? Did they describe how some so-called "safe investments" can drop during crashes? As a financial professional, did they explain how major crashes could devastate your savings and put your retirement at risk? Did he or she mention that you could see several crashes between now and your retirement?

Did they present a plan to protect your account?

From what I have heard from people who have spoken with other advisors, these issues are seldom discussed. Why? Because if you knew the facts about the stock market, you may not be so willing to invest.

So, with all this in mind, I have put together a list of six essential skills you should expect when choosing a financial professional. As I said earlier, they don't need to be your best friend, but they definitely need to have your best interests at heart. Here they are:

1. Long-Term Service
Interpersonal skills and communications. An excellent professional will maintain their relationship with you, will network with other associates, and will also be looking to grow their business and influence, so their people skills will be crucial. These include great email and telephone etiquette. They should keep in touch on a continuing basis, in good markets and in bad. Also, financial professionals often use acronyms and words that can confuse many investors. The best pros will explain these investment terms so you can make an informed decision. I find that gaining your trust will be just as important as maintaining your trust.

2. Keeping Calm Guidance During Crazy Markets
Like any job, stress will be inevitable. This is especially true when the markets are rattled. A true professional will be able to weather you through any storm if they take their responsibility seriously. This professionalism requires an exceptionally high level of focus and calm demeanor. A good financial professional will also understand that helping a client outweighs any amount of job stress.

3. Persistence and Hard Work
Although these skills are important for any profession, they are extremely valuable in the financial industry. The best financial professionals will stay on top of the investment market, will be up on the latest news coming out of Wall Street, be a good predictor of upcoming market trends, and understand what will be important to you.

4. Problem-Solving Skills

Every financial portfolio is unique and will require a different investment approach. A good financial professional will need to be patient under pressure and not react emotionally to the many market fluctuations. They also must have good mathematical skills and make prudent decisions based on long-term goals.

5. Passionate

I find it essential to be passionate about my job. I truly want to impact the lives of my clients and help them grow their wealth. I want to be the one who can take an insecure client with an insecure budget and make a positive difference in their retirement. I believe this approach is critical to my success in making a difference.

6. Organizational Skills

The last, and perhaps most important skill, is for a financial professional to be good at details. Not only does this help me grow my business, it also keeps me efficient in managing my clients. Being organized allows me to pay attention my clients' needs and eliminate mistakes that can be costly to them and my business. Being detail oriented also requires good cash flow planning, retirement planning, investment management, insurance planning, estate planning, and tax planning. All of these are important in helping clients.

I'll finish this chapter off by simply advising you to choose wisely. At last count there were over 200,000 financial advisors in the United States. Understandably, finding a perfect match can be difficult. But—and again, this is a big "but"—it could possibly be the most important decision of your life. As a financial professional, I just happen to believe it is.

Conclusion

21 Know Your Retirement Is Secure

Too many families go at it alone, with little to no financial education. Would you allow yourself to be operated on by a surgeon who did not attend medical school? Would you have an unlicensed electrician to wire your home? Both done wrong can have lasting negative consequences. Likewise, with financial planning.

> ***The more you know about financial planning,***
> ***the more you realize how much there is to know.***

You have worked decades to build your retirement accounts and your money may have to last 15, 20, 25 years or more. That's no small feat. Plan poorly, you may outlive your money and that's a scenario that I don't wish upon anyone.

Work with a financial professional so you can sleep well, knowing your retirement is secure.

> *With that, I wish you a prosperous,*
> *safe, and No-Stress Retirement!*
> —Scott

Endnotes

[1] www.wsj.com/ad/article/jh_secret_happy_retirement.html

[2] www.foxbusiness.com/markets/us-stocks-feb27-2020

[3] www.foxbusiness.com/markets/stocks-oil-fall-covid-19-black-friday-retail

[4] time.com/6186413/inflation-accelerates-40-year-high/

[5] www.foxbusiness.com/economy/98-percent-ceos-prepping-us-recession-survey

[6] www.nytimes.com/2022/02/01/us/politics/national-debt-30-trillion.html

[7] www.forbes.com/sites/mikepatton/2021/05/03/us-national-debt-expected-to-approach 89-trillion-by-2029

[8] In my life. Side 2 Track 3, Rubber Soul, Parlophone 1965, John Lennon, Paul McCartney (PAGE 29)

[9] www.cnbc.com/2017/01/04/a-brief-history-of-the-401k-which-changed-how-americans-retire.html

[10] Time, Why It's Time To Retire the 401(k), Stephen Gandel 10-19-2009

[11] thefiscaltimes.com/Columns/2016/03/04/Retirement-Revolution-Failed-Why-401k-Isn-t-Working

[12] www.economicpopulist.org/content/401k-scam

[13] www.oxfordreference.com/display/10.1093/acref/9780191826719.001.0001/q-oro-ed4-00016757

[14] www.goodreads.com/quotes/9325923-half-the-money-i-spend-on-advertising-is-wasted-the

[15] https://www.dashinvestments.com/wp-content/uploads/2015/11/MFCosts.pdf

[16] https://advisors.vanguard.com/strategies/fixed-income/active-fixed-income

If you like what you read, reach out.
We would love to hear from you.

WEALTH CONCEPTS
—— G R O U P ——

(832) 880-5555

www.WealthConceptsGroup.com